TEACHING WITH MUSIC THROUGH THE CHURCH YEAR

Judy Gattis Smith

A Griggs Educational Resource

Published by
Abingdon / Nashville

ISBN 0-687-41133-5

TABLE OF CONTENTS

Chapter

FOREWORD	1
INTRODUCTION	2
WAYS TO USE THIS BOOK	3
ADVENT AND CHRISTMASTIDE	
Cradle-Rocking Carols	5
Dancing Carols	8
Shepherd Carols	9
Legendary Carols	13
Snap, Clap and Tap Carols	17
Carols for Listening	18
Additional Ideas for Using Carols	18
Celebrate with Bells	19
EPIPHANY	
Using Our Hymnals	20
Getting Acquainted with your Hymnal	21
Epiphany Hymns	23
What Do Our Hymns say about Jesus?	27
Using Hymns to Intensify the meaning of Scripture	28
Using Church School Hymns in the Worship Service	29
LENT AND EASTER	
Listening to Music	30
Music in the Bible	30
Study what Hymns say about Death and Eternal Life	32
Events of Easter in song	32
Music in Children's Liturgy	36
Trumpet Sounds	36
Easter Bells	37
Hymns for Eastertide	38
Make Wind Chimes	38
Spring Songs	39

PENTECOST

Rhythmic Movement	40
Hands as Instruments	42
Rhythm Instruments	43
Use of Tambourines and Finger Cymbals	46
Jubal's Instruments	46
Visit an Organ	48
How did the first Christians Sing?	48
Youth and Music	49
How to Teach a Song — "We are the Church"	50

GOD THE CREATOR

Music for the very young Child	54
Finger songs	55
Music for the 3, 4, and 5 year old	55
Singing with Puppets	56
Music and Scripture cards	57
Art and Music	57
Music and Drama	61
Creative Writing and Music	64
Singing Games	66

CODA 66

FOREWORD

We are blessed here in this section of Virginia with the full range of seasons. As I sat at my desk working on this book the panorama outside my window has continually changed from the hesitant shyness of the first spring flowers to the tropical lushness and smothering heat of the Potomac River summer to the patchwork quilt of autumn trees to the stark whiteness of winter. I am aware of how much our appreciation of these seasons and the Creator God is intensified by the use of music. Can you imagine a silent Christmas with no carols ringing through the air? Can you imagine Easter without the blare of trumpets and the triumphant songs of resurrection? Can you imagine the herald of Spring without birds and children voices?

What is music? How did it first begin? Some say music was here before speech. Some say the first song was a mother crooning to her baby or primitive man's response to an unknown God. Music began so long ago its beginnings will be forever veiled in mystery. But music, whatever it is and however it began, has a language of its own through which God speaks to the human spirit. I believe music is an essential means of communicating the Christian faith and has an important place in Christian teaching.

So journey with me through the Church Year, through the church at learning and the church at worship. Raise your voices, clap your hands, play your instruments, set your feet dancing. Celebrate the seasons and celebrate our God!

Judy Gattis Smith
Arlington, Virginia

INTRODUCTION

A Look at the Role of Music in Christian Education

Music has two basic roles in Christian Education:

1. It should help a person grow in his understanding of God, of self and of others.
2. It should intensify a personal commitment to Christ and his church.

It is interesting to note how much our personal theology is shaped by music. In times of stress or crisis hymns often flash into our minds even before Scripture. If our musical growth has been stunted these may be childhood hymns or fantasy hymns that do not nourish us or give us solid foundations for adult lives. We have an important duty as teachers to provide students with a familiarity and understanding of good religious music as they build the structure of their faith. The words and thoughts expressed in music are important, but music is more than words. Its very tone, cadence and harmony speak of our faith to our spirits. All of the great movements, revolutions and religions of the world have been accompanied by music. Through music we reach a deeper level of commitment than words alone can express.

As teachers we need to remember the learning maxim that something set to music is easier to remember. Why do you think so many of our TV ads are jingles and songs? My husband, a mature person with a number of theological degrees, when asked to name the twelve disciples will revert to a song he learned in grammar school and sing:

"There were 12 disciples,
Jesus called to help him.
Simon, Peter, Andrew, James
and brother John"

For some people there is a mystique about music. Adults are sometimes frightened by its many technicalities. "I can't read music", they say, or "I can't sing". It is true that music can be a very complicated art requiring years of training but it can also be a simple, natural response of "making a joyful noise unto the Lord." As teachers we must earnestly strive to get rid of any hangups we may have about the difficulty of music and move on to the creation of the singing church. Music is a natural form of expression. Listen to the sounds a just-fed, new-born baby makes. It is music. The natural responses to rhythms and tones will develop happily in a child if we do not thwart them. First experiences in music should be times of exploration, experimentation and fun. Later comes sharing with others and working out ideas in a group.

A pamphlet published by the United Methodist Church states, "Adults working with children, planning together for ways in which children, through music may develop a mature concept of Christian living, will pass on to them a great heritage" ("The Role of Music in Christian Education").

How do we begin? A teacher might say, "We have choirs in our church. Isn't that enough?" In the first place, *most* of our children, youth and adults are not in choirs. Will we deny the non-choir persons religious musical experiences? Secondly, choirs are often concerned (though not wholly) with performance and perfecting of musical skills. *Our* task is learning and experiencing.

In this book we attempt to suggest ways of experiencing music through the church year, in learning centers and small groups, in congregational worship and intergenerational fellowships. There are experiences of an individual nature where each person examines his own feeling for rhythm and sound. There are experiences where the entire Christian community joins together singing, dancing, clapping.

I hope that this book will serve as a spark for your ideas. The teacher who is convinced that music is important and is personally enthusiastic about it will find ideas coming from many sources. It is an exciting experience to incorporate music into your teaching and, with your class, begin the creative process of "singing unto the Lord a new song". A brand new song. . . . .Your Very Own.

WAYS TO USE THIS BOOK

Churches use a variety of methods to teach. Music belongs in whatever method you use.

If you are the only teacher in a classroom the main responsibility to include music will be yours. This book can help you with ideas for learning songs, for using your hymnal, for planning together with your class for field trips related to music, for relating music to Scripture, art and drama. The musically untrained teacher in this setting may feel some qualms. Begin with some of the simplest musical experiences: clapping to records, playing rhythm instruments, chanting Psalms on one pitch. Encourage the students in your class to play and lead songs. Bring in parents with musical skills to help you. Ten simple ways to teach a song and the teaching of "We Are the Church" with 22 easy steps might be your next course of action. Self-expression can be to your advantage. You and your class are starting out together on equal footing on a musical adventure.

In team teaching two or more teachers work together to plan and lead the church school session. One of these teachers could have the main responsibility for music leadership and a person trained or particularly interested in this area could be chosen. In addition to the ideas suggested for the one-teacher class, this book offers suggestions to the team teacher for using rhythmic movement, singing games, a variety of ways to learn and use Christmas carols, projects such as making wind chimes and building an environment.

Some churches today are using the Learning Center approach to teaching. In this approach the room is set up with centers and children explore and learn at their own speed and according to their own interests and abilities. A music center is usually one of the parts of a learning center. This book offers suggestions for the purchase and use of a variety of instruments that can be a part of the Music Center (see the section "Jubal's Instruments" under Pentecost). There are also suggestions in the book for listening to music, and ideas for making instruments and experimenting individually with movement and sounds.

Some learning centers are set up for independent study where students are given instructions and then proceed without guidance from a teacher. This book offers such students suggestions for research on bells, for writing original songs and hymns, for comparing Scripture and hymns, for using a hymn evaluating chart and for studying music in the Bible.

One of the problems that leaders are discovering with learning centers is that there is little sense of community as each child works individually. One way to overcome this is with a good music leader. The entire group can be gathered together at the end of a learning center session and be joined together in song.

Another trend in Christian Education is toward intergenerational groups where plans are made purposefully to include people of varying ages. Again, music is ideal for this kind of interaction between persons. Some suggestions for intergenerational study in this book are: Look at what a variety of hymns say about Jesus, sponsor a church-wide bell festival, use instrumental groups of varying ages, dance in a circle to Christmas carols, play hymn charades, and, of course, sing together everything from prayers to fun songs to congregational singing. Music knows no age boundaries.

This book even includes suggestions for music for the one and two year old child!

The book also offers some suggestions for the use of music in the worship setting, for example, music in children's liturgy and the leadership of congregational singing by church school students. However, the main emphasis of the book is on music in the church school teaching situation.

As a teacher you should read through the entire book marking the ideas that would apply to your particular class, keeping in mind the age level and general setup.

Music, which is deeper and subtler in its effects than either language or logic, should play a vital role in Christian teaching whatever method you use.

The framework for this book is the Christian calendar. It is recognized that your particular church may use a slightly different division of the year. Some churches observe only Christmas and Easter. What we are trying to do is give a feel for the entire cycle of the church year and provide a foundation which assures balance and direction. Just as our calendar year moves from one season to another and we rejoice in the changes of the seasons so we move through the church year responding to the emphasis of the church seasons, avoiding sameness which can stifle and crush the Spirit.

However, do not feel bound by this framework. Some suggestions for one season work equally well at other times of the year. It is hoped that you will approach this book with freedom and creativity.

ADVENT AND CHRISTMAS

Just as in everyone's life certain days stand out from others, so it is in the Christian experience. Special days become a focal point for our worship. This is how the Christian year came to be. From the celebration of Jesus' birth, his death, and the beginning of the church, a cycle began to develop that gradually, over a period of time, came to be what we call the Church Year.

Attention naturally focused on the birth of Jesus. This watershed of history seemed to demand a special celebration—thus Christmas. The decision to settle on the date December 25 has a long and checkered history.

Soon the feeling began to develop that the momentous occasion of God coming to mankind through the birth of Christ demanded more than just one day's celebration. Christians felt they needed a period of time for the preparation of this celebration. A four-Sunday season preceding Christmas day was decided upon and this season became known as Advent. It is a season of joyful anticipation and this is the feeling we should try to capture in our church school music.

The entire church should be vibrating with music during this season. Choirs are preparing special music, radios in church offices are intoning carols and children, busy with Advent wreaths, are humming as they work. "There's a song in the air" is a most fitting description of the Christmas season. For everywhere that Christ's birth is honored it is celebrated in song.

In this section we will look particularly at Christmas carols and explore a number of ways they can be used in our teaching. Christmas carols offer a marvelous music resource for our church schools for several reasons:

1. They are easily obtainable in Christmas carol collections or standard hymnals.
2. They are already familiar to most people.
3. They can be used intergenerationally.
4. They can intensify a number of Christmas feelings.
5. They offer a variety of possibilities for use.

The first hymns in honor of the Nativity were written in the Fifth century soon after Christmas was fully established as one of the great annual church celebrations. These were in Latin, however, and it was not until the Thirteenth century, when St. Francis inspired his companions to write in their native tongue, that songs to celebrate the Nativity were written for the people to sing.

Christmas carols are of all types, from true folk songs to composed hymns. They come from all periods of time, from the Thirteenth century to the present.

The distinguishing note in carols is happiness. This makes even the oldest seem as modern and alive today as it was when it was first sung long ago.

A. CRADLE-ROCKING CAROLS

Some of our most beautiful carols are lullabies or cradle-rocking carols. A lovely custom called cradle-rocking (Kindelwiegen) originated in Germany and Austria about the 14th century. Two priests, one impersonating Mary, and the other Joseph, would rock an actual cradle as the people stood around them and joined in singing. Later the people were allowed to rock the cradle with their own hands. Some church historians say cradle-rocking was one of the things which enabled the church to make Christianity a genuinely popular religion in Germany.

Wouldn't this be a beautiful custom to revive in our Christmas worship services or in our church school classes? As children rock the cradle and lull the baby to sleep they can appreciate that the Christ Child is the "universal little brother of all the children on earth".

The very popular carol, "Away In A Manager" is an effective cradle-rocking song.

Even better fitted to this activity is the carol, "Joseph, Dearest Joseph Mine". This carol can easily be acted out in the manner of the 14th century Kindelwiegen with one child singing the first verse as Mary, another child singing the second verse as Joseph and the rest of the children in a circle around the cradle joining in the chorus and taking turns rocking the cradle.

JOSEPH, DEAREST JOSEPH MINE

Joseph, Dearest Joseph Mine, continued.

The Czech folk carol, ROCKING SONG may not be as familiar, but it works especially well with this activity and children love it.

ROCKING SONG—Same source as Joseph, Dearest Joseph mine.

As variations you could bring a rocking chair into your church school class and rock your young students or let them rock an imaginary baby Jesus as you sing. My daughter's first grade teacher had a rocking chair in her public school classroom. Whenever the day got rough for one of her young pupils she was never too busy to take time out for a "rocking". The Christmas season can become hectic and frantic for very young children. Our church school students may also benefit from a "rocking."

Still another way to use cradle-rocking carols is to have the students cradle their arms as though holding a baby and sway gently back and forth as they sing.

B. DANCING CAROLS

Although today the word, "carol", simply means a song that is sung at Christmas it originally meant a round dance. In the early days of Christianity dancing was a popular form of religious expression. As late as the Thirteenth and Fourteenth centuries there was always dancing in a circle around the creche in the churches of Europe on Christmas Eve. For many years the church frowned on dancing and when carols were finally accepted into the church it was the singing only—without dancing. Now dancing is coming into favor again and we are joyfully obeying the Psalm 150 command: "Praise him with the timbrel and dance."

Many of the Christmas carols beg to be danced. Historical precedence suggests a circle. It is interesting to note that when people first built homes they were often circular. The first group dances were circular and the early Christmas carol dances were also in a circle. This form can be used in our Church school classes and in our church worship. The group joins hands and does a simple step-skip-step, clockwise, as they sing together. This is an especially effective intergenerational way to experience the Christmas carols. "Joy to the World" danced in this manner by an entire congregation, young children dancing beside grandparents, is a glorious experience!

Other carols for jubilant dancing are:

Hark the Herald Angels Sing
Angels We Have Heard on High
Angels from the Realms of Glory
O Come, Little Children
O Thou Joyful Day
There's a Song in the Air
Lord of the Dance (Sydney Carter's modern dancing carol.)

If you feel uncomfortable trying this with a group, why not invite some persons who are experienced with dancing and singing to try it out in an experimental way? If it works for your experimental group then it will be much easier to implement in a larger gathering.

C. SHEPHERD CAROLS

The Nativity story as it is told in Luke's gospel is a very simple story: a world wide census was ordered which brought Mary and Joseph to Bethlehem where Mary brought forth her first born son. An angel announced to shepherds the news of great joy: the shepherds came to the stable, saw the child and spread the news.

This simple story has inspired countless variations with words, pictures, songs, dances and all types of drama. Prominent in these creative variations are the shepherds. They have been given names and ages and motives and personalities and have found their way into a number of beautiful Christmas carols.

Identifying with the shepherds through some of our Christmas carols can be a meaningful experience in our church school. Though our surroundings are more likely urban than pastoral, we can imagine the Christmas setting with shepherds on the hillside piping of the joys and sorrows of life.

Recorders and flutes lend themselves beautifully to these pastoral songs. In many public schools the recorder is taught and your students may be able to play the melody line as the class sings along. Or, use a student flutist or a member of the church or community who plays the flute to lead you in these shepherd songs.

Following are instructions for a Music Learning Center plan on the theme of Shepherd carols, to be a part of a larger Christmas learning center. This learning center plan is based on the assumption that students have free choice of activities. Four activities are suggested in the Music Center: Learning Shepherd Carols, Studying a Shepherd Spiritual, Pantomiming to Song, Writing a Shepherd Carol. Students may complete one or all of these activities. Activity 2 helps the student discover facts and ideas, activities 1, 3 and 4 stress expression and creativity.

A Music Learning Center Plan For Shepherd Carols

1. Carols about shepherds are mounted on pieces of poster paper and marked for use with tone blocks or autoharp. Carols to use include:

   Come, All Ye Shepherds
   It Came Upon the Midnight Clear
   O Little Town of Bethlehem
   Shepherds! Shake Off your Drowsy Sleep
   Silent Night
   While Shepherds Watched their Flocks

2. Rise Up, Shepherds, and Follow. On the wall is a poster with this heading and these instructions:

   Read the words to this Negro Spiritual

   There's a star in the East on Christmas morn,
   Rise up, shepherd, and follow!
   It will lead to the place where the Saviour's born
   Rise up, shepherd, and follow!
   Leave your sheep and leave your lambs;
   Rise up, shepherd, and follow!
   Leave your ewes and leave your rams;
   Rise up, shepherd, and follow!

   Follow! Follow!
   Rise up, shepherd, and follow!
   Follow the star to Bethlehem
   Rise up, shepherd, and follow.

Read the Christmas story from the Bible:
Matt. 2:1-12 and Luke 2:8-20

Compare the accounts by answering the following questions:

a. Who followed the star?
   In the Spiritual ____________________
   In Matthew ____________________
   In Luke ____________________

b. Which tells about shepherds?
   In the Spiritual ____________________
   In Matthew ____________________
   In Luke ____________________

c. When did the star appear?
   In the Spiritual ____________________
   In Matthew ____________________

You have discovered that the details of the Nativity story are not accurately presented in this carol. This happens in many carols from various countries. Discuss with your adult leader: If accuracy is not the main purpose of this Spiritual, what do you think *is* the main purpose?

3. Provide a box with shepherd costumes marked "Try Me On". Instructions:

   Read the words to "Shepherds Come A Running" or listen to them on tape or record.

   See if you can do what the song tells you to do. In costume, act out the song without using words. Can you pantomime anxious hurrying, giving of very simple gifts, piping or dancing for the Christ?

   Find a friend to act out the carol with you.

SHEPHERDS COME A-RUNNING

3. Merrily the shepherds all are dancing round,
Shepherds singing, sheep bells ringing, pipes gayly sound!
Deeply now they bow to Mary, singing farewell to the Child,
Tiny Child:
Deeply now they bow to Mary, singing farewell to the Child,
Jesus mild.

4. Write your own shepherd carol. Use a familiar tune or make up your own. Give your shepherds names, ages and personalities.

D. LEGENDARY CAROLS

Some of our carols, springing from the fertile imagination of the common people, stray far from the facts of the original Nativity story but personalize the Christmas story in a refreshing way. People living in cold, bleak, climates have given us carols about pine trees and snow. From southern countries come carols telling of birds and flowers. Hill people have given us carols of hill animals and their keepers, and persons living in lands facing the sea have given us carols about ships carrying precious cargo. These legendary carols are usually pure folk songs handed down by singing from one generation to another.

One of the most interesting of these carols is the traditional English carol, "I Saw Three Ships"

I saw three ships come sailing in,
On Christmas Day, on Christmas Day.
I saw three ships come sailing in,
On Christmas Day in the morning.

And what was in those ships all three,
On Christmas Day, on Christmas Day,
And what was in those ships all three,
On Christmas Day in the morning?

The Virgin Mary and Christ were there,
On Christmas Day, on Christmas Day,
The Virgin Mary and Christ were there,
On Christmas Day in the morning.

Pray, whither sailed those ships all three,
On Christmas Day, on Christmas Day,
Pray, whither sailed those ships all three,
On Christmas Day in the morning?

O they sailed into Bethlehem,
On Christmas Day, on Christmas Day,
O they sailed into Bethlehem,
On Christmas Day in the morning.

Many think this carol originated in Cornwall, England, where the people's lives are influenced by the surrounding sea. The mists which rise from the coast and the moors in this area further add an air of mystery and it is possible to imagine all sorts of things coming from the sea. That Bethlehem was not a seaport town presents no problem. The author of this charming and ingenuous carol lived in the world of imagination rather than facts.

Learn this carol with your church school class and then use it as a basis for writing an original carol.

Step 1. Think about the area in which you live. What is distinctive about it? What is the weather at Christmas? What are the fauna and flora? Brainstorm and list all of these facts on the board.

Step 2. Try to imagine the Nativity event taking place right in the area where you live. What might be equivalent to the stable? Who, from your community, might come to the manger? What might they bring? List these ideas.

Step 3. Now, using this information create your own carol using "I Saw Three Ships" as your basic form.

For example, here in Arlington, Virginia, on the outskirts of Washington, D.C. the children wrote:

I saw three Senators coming in,
On Christmas Day, on Christmas Day.
I saw three Senators coming in,
On Christmas Day in the morning.

They went to the White House, bright and gay,
On Christmas Day, on Christmas Day.
They went to the White House, bright and gay,
On Christmas Day in the morning.

But where did the baby Jesus lay?
On Christmas Day, on Christmas Day.
But where did the baby Jesus lay?
On Christmas Day in the morning.

He lay in a motel far from town,
On Christmas Day, on Christmas Day.
He lay in a motel far from town,
On Christmas Day in the morning.

He lay in a motel quite run down,
On Christmas Day, on Christmas Day.
He lay in a motel quite run down,
On Christmas Day in the morning.

Other legendary carols that fascinate children (and some of us adults) are carols in which birds, animals and bees speak and sing, trees leaf and flowers blossom in the snows of winter. It is fun for students to create masks out of paper sacks to wear as they act out these carols. Use brown grocery bags, size No. 20. Cut out eyes for each student and let them decorate their own masks, with crayons or tempera paints. They might wish to add feathers cut from construction paper. The French carol, CAROL OF THE BIRDS is good to use for this activity. Students can create masks of roosters, goldfinches, sparrows, blackbirds, pigeons, larks, greenfinches, wagtails, nightingales, quails or imaginary birds. It might be helpful to have some bird books on hand to help spark the student's creativity. After completing the masks the song can be sung or played as the students freely act it out.

CAROL OF THE BIRDS
Le Nöel des Oiseaux

A BOOK OF CHRISTMAS CAROLS Selected and Illustrated by Haig and Regina Shekerjian.

2. In stable bare lies baby sweet;
Brown ox and donkey guard his sleep.
Why, little birds, did you come too?
"We bring love to Him, Jesu."

3. Up from the hay, flew rooster old,
Up to the rack, he flew most bold,
Crowing a blessing clear and true,
Crowing so clear: "Coucouroucou!"

4. Down from his nest the goldfinch flew,
Bowed and said: "Tirli, chiu, chiu!"
"Chiu, chiu!" replied the sparrow small,
And the quail called: "Palpabat-bal!"

5. Whistling lightly, blackbird comes,
While the linnet softly hums;
Pigeon calls: "Roucou, roucou!"
And the lark sings: "Tirolirou!"

6. Perching beside the greenfinch small,
Wagtail does sing and sweetly call;
While nightingale up in the tree
Sings to the Child: "La sol fa mi!"

7. To honor Him, the child Jesu,
Angels and shepherds, sweet birds too,
Come and adore Him, your love tell;
Sing Noël! Noël! Noël!

2. Dans l'étable où le Roi du Ciel
Dort entre l'âne et le boeuf brun,
Pourquoi venez-vous donc, oiseaux?
"Nous venons pour adorer Dieu!"

3. Le coq s'avance le permier,
Et monte sur le râtelier,
Puis, pour commencer l'oraison,
Il entonn' son: "Coucouroucou!"

4. Le chardonn'ret sort de son nid,
Salue et dit: "Tirli, chiu, chiu!"
"Chiu, chiu!" répond le passereau,
Et la caille fait: "Palpabat!"

5. Le merle arrive en sifflotant,
Et le linot en chantonnant;
Le pigeon fait: "Roucou, roucou!"
Et l'alouett': "Tirolirou!"

6. La bergeronnette, à son tour,
Se pose a côté du verdier,
Et, sur l'arbre, le rossignol
Chante à l'Enfant: "Ré mi fa sol!"

7. Pour honorer le fils de Dieu,
Venez en grande dévotion,
Anges, bergers, oiseaux, du Ciel,
Chantez Noël! Noël! Noël!

Another good carol to use with masks is "The Friendly Beasts". Many old legends tell us of the gift of speech given to animals on the night that Christ was born. These friendly beasts talk happily together of their participation in the events of that wonderful night.

Jesus, our brother kind and good
Was humbly born in a stable rude.
The friendly beasts around Him stood,
Jesus, our brother, kind and good,

"I", said the donkey, all shaggy and brown,
"I carried His mother uphill and down,
I carried her safely to Bethlehem town."
"I", said the donkey, all shaggy and brown.

"I", said the cow, all white and red,
"I gave Him my manger for a bed,
I gave Him my hay to pillow His head."
"I", said the cow, all white and red.

"I", said the sheep with the curly horn,
"I gave Him my wool for a blanket warm,
He wore my coat on Christmas morn."
"I", said the sheep with the curly horn.

"I", said the dove from the rafters high,
"I cooed Him to sleep so He would not cry,
We cooed Him to sleep, my mate and I"
"I", said the dove from the rafters high.

So every beast, by some good spell,
In the stable rude was glad to tell
Of the gift he gave Immanuel,
The gift he gave Immanuel.

English carol

Words attributed to Robert Davis

E. SNAP, CLAP AND TAP CAROLS

Probably the largest store of indigenous Christmas music in the United States grows out of the tradition of the Black Americans. Many of these spirituals have strong rhythmic forms and are good carols to accompany by snapping fingers, clapping hands and tapping feet.

Students enjoy accumulative songs such as "The Twelve Days Of Christmas". A spiritual that rivals this popular Christmas song is "Children, Go Where I Send You" and they are sent out "Two-by Twos", "Three-by Threes" etc.

It is interesting how the form of our Black carols closely resembles the carole of the Middle Ages: the frequent use of a choral refrain alternating with stanzas lined out by a leader. The form also makes the songs quick and easy to learn. Some beautiful Black carols for your class to learn are:

Rise Up, Shepherd, and Follow
My Lord, What a Morning!
Wasn't That a Mighty Day
Mary Had a Baby
Oh, Jerus'lem in the Morning!

Go, Tell It on the Mountains
Poor Little Jesus
Behold That Star
The Little Cradle Rocks Tonight
Sister Mary Had But One Child
What You Gonna Call Yo' Pretty Little Baby?

Music for guitar and piano and words for all these songs can be found in THE SEASON FOR SINGING compiled by John Langstaff, Doubleday and Co., Garden City, N.Y., 1974.

F. CAROLS FOR LISTENING

In the busy Christmas season not only should students have time for singing old favorites and for learning new carols, but time should also be set aside for listening. There are many recordings of Christmas music available from stores and libraries and home collections. Perhaps you could locate some different carols for your students to hear. There are recordings of American Colonial Christmas music with original instruments and collections of Moravian or Shaker Christmas music. Perhaps your class would enjoy Christmas folk songs from Appalachia. Or, you might want to have one of the lovely recordings of Handel's MESSIAH for students to love while growing into it. The PASTORAL SYMPHONY or a chorus from this work makes good listening music.

One teacher of 5th and 6th grade students taught her class the soprano line of the text, "Wonderful, Counselor, the Mighty God, the Everlasting Father, the Prince of Peace." It appears four times in the chorus "For Unto Us a Child is Born" from the MESSIAH. The class listened to a record of this chorus hearing the preceding words, "For unto us a child is born; unto us a Son is given. And the government shall be upon His shoulder and His name shall be called. . .". . . . . . .and here the class joined joyfully in the line they had learned.

G. CHRISTMAS CAROLING

Bringing the joy of Christmas to others through Christmas carols is a wonderful way to celebrate the Season. But sometimes this happy tradition has a sameness about it that gets boring. Try singing your carols in new locations. Traveling is a lonely experience at Christmastime. What about taking your carolers to greet incoming busses or trains or airplanes? Have you ever brought the warmth of the Christmas spirit to lonely hotel dwellers and travelers by singing in hotel and motel lobbies? City dwellers enjoy carolers in the lobbies of apartment buildings or in shopping centers or outside busy department stores.

We usually remember those in hospitals and nursing homes at this time (and we should) but it is also nice to take your carolers to people who are not expecting it. What about singing at the homes of some of your church officials such as board chairman, president of your women's group, your lay leaders, etc. They would be delightfully surprised and your students would see a larger dimension of the church.

Consider a variety of ways to go caroling. Rent a bus and sing out the windows, pile into the back of a truck, or have a walking candle-light procession. (If going by bus or truck be sure to arrange for insurance coverage.)

With the purpose of intensifying the spirit of Christmas for others, the possibilities for places, people and modes of transportation are endless.

H. ADDITIONAL IDEAS FOR USING CAROLS

1. Study the stories of how carols came to be written. The story of the writing of SILENT NIGHT is a lovely one for children to act out. They can end by singing the carol to guitar accompaniment as it was first written.

2. Look up the origins of carols and group them by nationalities. Learn the carols of different countries. For example, here is a grouping of some of our most familiar carols:

England: Hark the Herald Angels Sing
Joy to the World
What Child is This?

France:	Bring a Torch, Jeanette, Isabella The First Noel O Holy Night
Germany:	Silent Night O Christmas Tree O Come Little Children
United States:	O Little Town of Bethlehem We Three Kings It Came Upon A Midnight Clear

3. Use carols to add atmosphere to your other Christmas activities. For example, sing "Deck The Halls" as you decorate your classroom for Christmas. Sing "O Christmas Tree" as you decorate the tree.

I. CELEBRATE WITH BELLS

In addition to the Christmas carols, the bright ringing of bells is another musical sound we associate with the Christmas season. There are a variety of ways these sparkling instruments can be used in the church school:

1. Small children can perform as "reindeer" wearing small bells tied to their ankles and wrists as they sing "Jingle Bells" or prance about to Christmas records.
2. Older children can sponsor a bell festival asking everyone in the church or classroom to bring a bell for display. Look for the most unique, the biggest bell, the smallest bell, the one with the most interesting story.
3. Learn the carol, "I Heard The Bells On Christmas Day" and ring bells as you sing.

Suggestions for Learning Centers.

1. Make egg carton bells (see directions in TEACHING AND CELEBRATING ADVENT by Patricia and Donald Griggs)
2. Do research on the high priests of the ancient Hebrews. Why did they wear robes decorated with tiny, golden bells and why did they ring hand bells at their ceremonies? Make an illustration of these ceremonial robes. Have books on hand, such as BIBLE ENCYCLOPEDIA FOR CHILDREN, by Cecil Northcott, Westminster press, to aid in this research.
3. Do research on bells in Christian churches. When did they first appear? Why were they given names? The pealing of Church bells in medieval times was said to drive away lightning and purify the air after an epidemic. Can you find other examples of powers these Middle Ages bells were supposed to have? A good book to help in this research is: ONE THOUSAND AND ONE CHRISTMAS FACTS AND FANCIES, by Alfred Carl Hottes; Dodd, Mead and Co., 1944. Also consult Encyclopedias.

Field Trip

Visit a carillon with your class if it is possible. A carillon has as many as 70 bells and is played from a keyboard. Two of the most famous in our country are found at the Singing Tower in Florida at Lake Wales and at Riverside Church in New York City.

With happiness, joyful anticipation and a song in the air, Christmas can become a more meaningful season for your students.

EPIPHANY

Wedged between the celebration of Jesus' birth and of his death and resurrection, is the season of Epiphany. This beautiful season sometimes gets lost in the aftermath of Christmas. The word "Epiphany" means "manifestation" and refers to Christ manifesting himself as our Divine Savior. It is a fixed date festival always occurring on January 6 and is associated with the birth and baptism of Jesus and the visit of the Magi.

Although we celebrate Epiphany on January 6 the season itself lasts until Lent. The theme of telling the good news of Christ to all the world, illustrated by Magi, makes this a season where Missions are emphasized in some of our churches.

One of our best sources of music for our classes to use in the season of Epiphany, is our hymnal. This section of the book will look first at how to use the hymnal as a teaching tool, and then, how to use some of the more familiar Epiphany hymns in a learning setting.

A. USING OUR HYMNALS

This book is intended to be read by all Christians. As we think of hymn singing we are aware that though many of our hymns are similar, many are also very different. Our topic of hymn singing is further complicated by the fact that within individual denominations there is often a wide variety of types of hymns that are sung.

I do not subscribe to the opinion of some musicians that there are "good" hymns (those which exhibit harmonic variety and chord progression, for example) and "bad" hymns (a weak tune with little harmony change, for example). I do not feel we can use a single standard for judging all hymns. If our purpose is to make a joyful noise unto the Lord, and try to grow through music in our understanding of God and our dedication to him, there is no place for musical snobbery. Of course we want good theology, good poetry and good music but this must always be balanced with an understanding of the persons involved and a sensitivity to their cultural background and present needs.

How then, do we go about choosing hymns? We begin with self-understanding. We should be aware of where our class or congregation is and where they are capable of going in the expression of their faith in song. As teachers we should not select hymns that express only our views, but should also seek to express views of others which may be different from our own. For example, older persons may be deeply moved by a hymn such as "I Am Thine, O Lord," and a group of teenagers may be equally moved by "They Will Know We Are Christians By Our Love."

Second, we should look at the context in which the hymn is being used. What is its function? The use of "Come Thou Almighty King" in a very formal worship setting serves an entirely different function than the singing of "Joy, Joy, Joy, Joy, Down In My Heart" with young children in a Vacation Church School setting.

For some years I have found the following chart helpful in evaluating hymns. I am sorry that I do not know its original source. Use this with your students to help determine where they are musically.

1. Select a hymn, popular with your group.
2. Sing it together.
3. Working individually, answer all the questions on the chart.
4. Compare answers. A lively discussion should follow.
5. Use the chart again. This time with an unfamiliar hymn.

GUIDE FOR EVALUATION OF HYMNS

Read the question and then circle the response which you think is appropriate for the hymn you are evaluating.

Questions	Responses
1. What concepts of God does the hymn express?	Loving Father Stern Judge Far Removed Near His people Father of all mankind Other
2. Are the concepts presented in this hymn appropriate for the age student you are teaching and consistent with the purpose of the lesson?	Fairly so Yes No
3. What feelings does the hymn arouse in you?	Worship Majesty Humility Joy Praise Irritation
4. What ideas about life does the hymn express?	Present life Future life Has no bearing on life problems
5. Is the meaning of the hymn clear?	Yes No
6. What kind of tune is used?	Dignified Joyous Sentimental Jazzy
7. Is the music suited to the words?	Yes No
8. Can the hymn be sung without strain on the voice?	Yes No Not by Children Not by Adults
9. To which of the following age groups is the hymn suited?	Nursery-Kindergarten Primary (6-8 yr. olds) Juniors (9-11 yr. olds) Intermediates (12-15 yr. olds) Older Youth (16 yr. and up) Adults

B. GETTING ACQUAINTED WITH YOUR HYMNAL

Just as our primary job in teaching the Bible is to serve as translators, so must we be translators of the hymnal to our students. From the third grade, when our students begin to read well, the particular hymnal of your denomination should be an important part of their musical experience.

The first thing that children must be taught is how to follow the words of any given stanza from line to line. Explain to your students that we go across the first line. Then, instead of reading the next line directly underneath, in a hymnal, we come down to the next group of lines and read there. Perhaps it is wise to teach a hymn without the book first so their first look at the book will be a pleasurable experience of recognition.

When the children feel comfortable with singing from the hymnal there are a number of other items that you will need to help translate. They will need to become familiar with the different indexes: topical, first line, tune, composer and author. They will need to learn to use the metrical index to find alternate tunes for hymn texts.

A game approach is a good way to teach this information.

1. Look first at the hymn title. Often the title is the same as the first line of the hymn. The purpose of the title is to make it easier to refer to the hymn. Perhaps your students can suggest other uses of the title. Turn with your students to the First-Line Index. This includes the first lines of all the hymns included in the book. Call out the name of a hymn and see which student can find the correct page number first. This is a good index to begin with because you can use hymns the students have already sung, then introduce new ones.

2. To find their way around in the hymnal the students need to become familiar with the main sections. They should be able to find the hymns of praise and the hymns for various seasons. This information is sometimes found in the Table of Contents and sometimes in the Topical Index. Choose a topic which correlates with your lesson for the day and find the appropriate hymns. For example, if you are studying "worship" a look at the hymns of praise would be helpful. Sing a number of these and try to get a "feel" for what they are saying about worship. If the season is Lent, find the section that includes all the Lenten hymns. Read their titles or first lines and your students will get a good idea of the theological emphasis of this season.

3. Two names appear at the top of the hymn. Ask your students who they think these people are and why their names are here. They will probably answer: Author and Composer. Which is which? The name of the author of the text and his dates are listed at the left of a hymn. The name of the composer of the tune is listed at the right. (remember that A comes before C in the alphabet and you have it.) There is usually an index listing authors and all of their works which are included in your hymnal and also an index of composers and all of their works. When you are studying a particular hymn look at the names of author and composer. Have students find out who was the older, the author or the composer. Then have them look in their indexes to see if there are other songs that they know by the same composer. In our United Methodist hymnal we always look up Charles and John Wesley and, seeing the large number of hymns they wrote, comment on our heritage as "singing Methodists". This index is also helpful in seeing if there are new hymns in your hymnal. Just look at the dates of the composer and author.

4. Hymn tune titles are usually underneath the title. This refers to the music and you will find an alphabetical index of these tunes in the front or back of your hymnal. Looking at this index you discover that two or three references are given for some of the tunes. For example, in ARMED FORCES HYMNAL the tune "Adeste Fideles" may be sung with the words "O Come All Ye Faithful," No. 188, or "How Firm A Foundation," No. 304. Julain's DICTIONARY OF HYMNOLOGY and Bailey's GOSPEL IN HYMNS are good resources if you are interested in finding out how hymn tunes got their names.

5. What are those strange numbers or letters after the hymn-tune title? Is this some secret code known only to musicians and editors of hymnals? Not at all. It is a code, but not too secret. Flip through the hymnal and have students call out the letters they find. List these on the board. Keep looking until all of these combinations are found:

   S.M. C.M. L.M. S.M.D. C.M.D. L.M.D.

   These letters tell how many lines in each stanza and how many syllables in each line. S.M. stands for short meter which counts out 6 syllables to the first line of the hymn, 6 to the second, 8 to the third and 6 to the fourth. (6.6.8.6.): C.M. is common meter (8.6.8.6) and L.M. is long meter (8.8.8.8.). The D. simply means double, in other words, repeat the meter pattern.

   Whenever one of these regular meter patterns will not fit a particular hymn poem, numbers alone are used to indicate the number syllables. Take a familiar hymn, such as "Holy Holy Holy" and have the students count together the number of syllables in the first line.

   Ho ly Ho ly Ho ly Lord God Al might y — 11 syllables

   The second line:

   Ear ly in the morn ing our song shall rise to thee — 12 syllables

   Third line:

   Ho ly Ho ly Ho ly Mer ci ful and migh ty — 12 syllables

Fourth line:

God in three per sons bless ed trin i ty — 10 syllables.

Thus the meter for this hymn is 11.12.12.10. It is not one of the regular meters.

Now, using meter and the metrical index the students can sing hymns to different tunes. They can find hymns that have the same metrical rhythm but different words.

6. When the group is familiar with the hymnal a treasure hunt can be used to reinforce their learning. Pick out a hymn and give a clue (such as the name of the composer). Clue 2 might be the metrical rhythm of the hymn. Continue with clues until someone finds the correct hymn. The hymn number might be your final clue. This game would make an interesting activity for an intergenerational group.

7. Other games might be: mimeographed sheets of true-false questions about the hymnal, games matching tunes and text, crossword puzzles using titles of hymns and authors and composers. For a hard game try playing snatches of hymns for identification or clap the rhythm of a hymn and see if the class can identify it.

C. EPIPHANY HYMNS

No hymns or carols are more dramatic than the ones about the Wiseman. These hymns call for performance and experiencing as well as singing.

"We Three Kings Of Orient Are" is probably the most familiar of our Wisemen hymns. Many authorities would name this Christmas hymn as the best to come out of America.

Verse 1

We three kings of Orient are:
Bearing gifts we traverse afar
Field and fountain, moor and mountain,
Following yonder star.

Chorus:

O star of wonder, star of night
Star with royal beauty bright,
Westward leading, still proceeding,
Guide us to thy perfect light.

Verse 2 Gaspar

Born a King on Bethlehem's plain,
Gold I bring to crown him again,
King forever, ceasing never
Over us all to reign.

(repeat chorus)

Verse 3 Melchior

Frankincense to offer have I,
Incense owns a Deity nigh;
Prayer and Praising, all men raising,
Worship Him, God on high.

(repeat chorus)

Verse 4 Balthasar:

Myrrh is mine; its bitter perfume
Breathes a life of gathering gloom;
Sorrowing, sighing, bleeding, dying,
Sealed in the stone-cold tomb.

(repeat chorus)

Verse 5

Glorious now behold him arise,
King and God and sacrifice:
Alleluia, Alleluia!
Earth to the heavens replies.

(repeat chorus)

Words and music by John H. Hopkins, Jr.

There are several ways to add a dramatic touch to this hymn:

1. Three students could sing the roles of the three Magi in verses 2, 3, and 4. Everyone sings the first and last verses and the choruses.
2. The class could march in follow-the-leader style in a swaying stately procession to the hymn on record or singing.
3. Seated in their chairs, students could stamp their feet in imitation of the steady, sure steps of the camels throughout the singing of the carol.
4. Finger cymbals could be used to represent the camel bells sounding in rhythm to their walk and hand drums could set the slow, processional march tempo.

D. AS WITH GLADNESS MEN OF OLD

Another hymn capturing the message of Epiphany is AS WITH GLADNESS MEN OF OLD.

For individual work with this hymn:

1. Read Matthew 2:1-11. Compare with this hymn.
2. List the reasons that this is a good Epiphany hymn.
3. What does it mean to tell the "Good News"? How could you tell the "Good News" to someone this week? Who would you tell and what would you tell?
4. List as many ways as you can think of for your church to celebrate Epiphany.

Step 1: Read Psalm 90:1-6, 12 in several translations.

From **Today's English Version:**

Lord, you have always been our home.
Before the hills were created,
before you brought the world into being,
you are eternally God, without beginning or end.
You tell men to return to what they were;
you change them back to soil.
A thousand years to you are like one day;
they are like yesterday, already gone,
like a short hour in the night.
You carry men away like a flood;
they last no longer than a dream.
They are like weeds that sprout in the morning,
that grow and burst into bloom,
then dry up and die in the evening.

Teach us how short our life is,
so that we may become wise.

From the **Revised Standard Version:**

Lord, thou hast been our dwelling place in all generations,
Before the mountains were brought forth,
or ever thou hadst formed the earth and the world,
from everlasting to everlasting thou art God.

Thou turnest man back to the dust,
and sayest, "Turn back, O children of men!"
For a thousand years in thy sight
are but as yesterday when it is past,
or as a watch in the night.

Thou dost sweep men away; they are like a dream,
like grass which is renewed in the morning;
in the morning it flourishes and is renewed;
in the evening it fades and withers.

So teach us to number our days
that we may get a heart of wisdom.

From the **King James Version:**

Lord, thou hast been our dwelling place in all generations.
Before the mountains were brought forth, or ever thou hadst formed the earth and the world, even from everlasting to everlasting thou art God.
Thou turnest man to destruction; and sayest, "Return, ye children of men."
For a thousand years in thy sight are but as yesterday when it is past, and as a watch in the night.
Thou carriest them away as with a flood; they are as a sleep; in the morning they are like grass which groweth up.
In the morning it flourisheth, and groweth up; in the evening it is cut down, and withereth.
So teach us to number our days, that we may apply our hearts unto wisdom.

Step 2: Read the words of the hymn "O God, Our Help in Ages Past."

Step 3: Compare the hymn with the Psalm. Where are they similar? Where are they different?

Step 4:	Write your own translation of this Psalm in your own words.
Step 5:	Share your writing with a teacher or other student.

Coordinating Scripture with hymns is an activity which can enrich our singing and our classes from 3rd grade up. Look up the Scripture that is included in your curriculum lesson for the day and see if there is a hymn to go along with it. Many hymnals have a section in the front or back for the specific purpose of coordinating hymns and Scripture. This can even become a game for students. Give them a Scripture passage and see if they can find hymns, in their hymnal, that match the Scripture passage.

F. IN CHRIST THERE IS NO EAST OR WEST

IN CHRIST THERE IS NO EAST NOR WEST

JOHN OXENHAM, 1852-1941

ST. PETER CM
ALEXANDER R. REINAGLE, 1799-1877

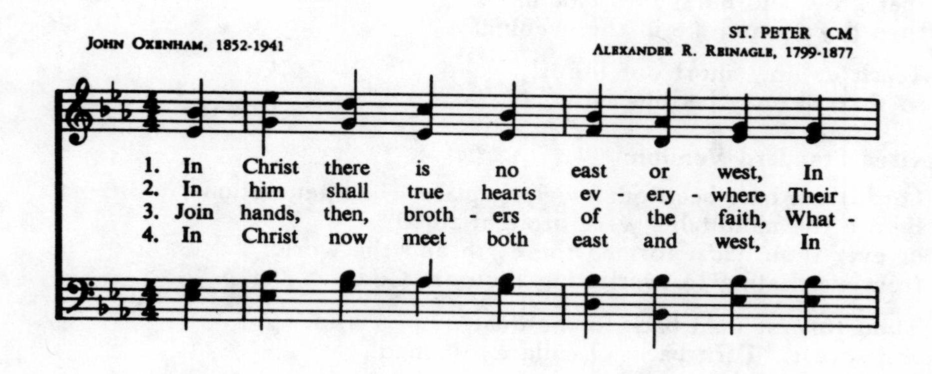

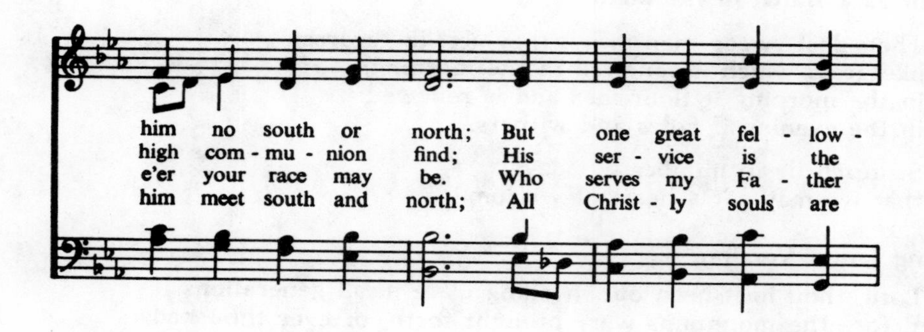

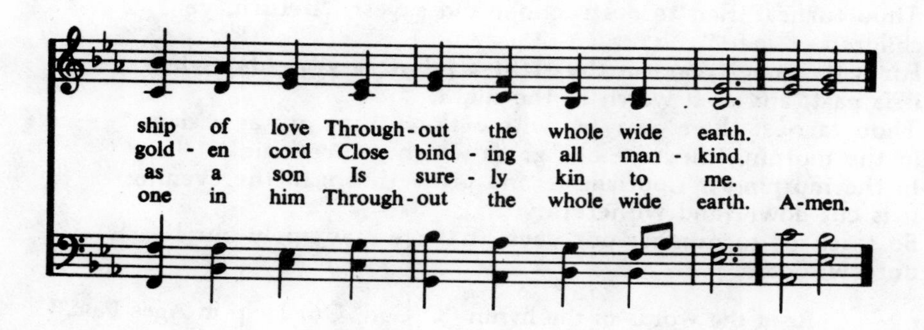

By permission

This is a hymn that captures the outreach and mission emphasis of the Epiphany season. It is an excellent hymn to interpret with creative movement.

After learning the hymn ask the students what they can do in the way of movement with the words of the hymn. How can we interpret it with our bodies? Gradually students will develop a good bit of originality in response as they go through the hymn.

To begin creative movement to this hymn you might suggest the interpretation as given by Margaret Fisk Taylor in her book, THE ART OF THE RHYTHMIC CHOIR. She suggests it be done in the following manner:

> The group forms a circle and numbers off "ones and twos". Then the group joins hands for the first stanza. (see above). The group simply moves around the "whole earth" walking in a circle with hands joined. Then the ones and twos face each other in pairs for the next stanza. They then do, in square dance terms, a Grand Right and Left, to the second stanza. On the last stanza the ones simply step out away from the twos and step inside to form an inner circle. They join hands and lift their arms up high. Then the twos from the outer circle join hands and on the last line of the hymn the outside circle comes under the arms of the inside circle, the arms of the inner circle now around the backs of the others.

This way of doing the hymn is only one suggestion. Your main job as teacher is to bring out the group's interpretation. (More on rhythmic movement under Pentecost).

The use of the hymnal, of course, should not be confined just to the season of Epiphany. It is our basic music textbook in our church school. Following are more suggestions for using the hymnal. Though included in the season of Epiphany, they would be appropriate during any season of the year.

G. WHAT DO OUR HYMNS SAY ABOUT JESUS?

An interesting and helpful intergenerational or class activity is to look at what a variety of hymns say about Jesus.

For this activity you will need a piano accompanist and hymnals for each person, paper and pencils.

Using your own hymnal, select a number of hymns that picture Jesus in a variety of ways.

For example, from the United Methodist Hymnal:

- Dear Master, In Whose Life I See
- All Hail the Power of Jesus' Name
- Fairest Lord Jesus
- Thou Hidden Source of Calm Repose
- Saviour Like a Shepherd Lead Us
- O Holy Saviour, Friend Unseen
- O Young and Fearless Prophet
- Soldiers of Christ Arise
- What a Friend We Have in Jesus
- What Child is This?
- O Come, O Come Emmanuel
- Hail to the Lord's Anointed
- Strong Son of God
- O Master Workman of the Race
- In Christ There is No East or West
- Stand Up, Stand Up for Jesus

Ask the class to sing a hymn together and then jot down one word that describes how Jesus is pictured in the hymn. Move on to the next hymn and follow the same procedure.

The number of hymns to be used should be determined by your time schedule and the sustained interest of the group. You may want to use a soloist on occasional hymns to give the group a singing rest.

Some suggested activities after several hymns have been sung:

1. Make a composite list of all the key words that are descriptive of Jesus. Select the words that students think best describe Jesus from his/her point of view.
2. Find a passage in one of the gospels that expresses a similar image of Jesus. Use a Concordance and the Scripture reference section of the hymnal as resources to help with this.
3. Select a teaching picture and/or a photograph to express visually the image of Jesus that is presented in the hymn.
4. Students could select a favorite hymn about Jesus and create their own paintings, drawings, slides or poems to communicate their impressions of Jesus.

H. USE HYMNS TO INTENSIFY THE MEANING OF SCRIPTURE

Often a passage of Scripture will fall on ears deafened by familiarity. Music can be used to help us hear the words again in a fresh way and can intensify their meaning for us.

For example, Galatians 5:22-23 "But the fruit of the Spirit is love, joy, peace, patience, kindness, goodness, faithfulness, gentleness, self-control."

Take the nine qualities mentioned in this passage and sing a hymn illustrating each quality. Check your church's hymnal to see if similar hymns can be found. You may have other hymns you wish to substitute for those suggested.

LOVE
More Love to Thee, O Christ

JOY
Joyful, Joyful, We Adore Thee

PEACE
Peace, Perfect Peace

PATIENCE
O Master, Let Me Walk with Thee

KINDNESS
Blest Be the Tie that Binds

GOODNESS
I Would be True

FAITHFULNESS
Faith of Our Fathers

GENTLENESS
How Gentle God's Commands

SELF-CONTROL
He Who Would Valiant Be

This method of study can be used effectively with youth and adults. Other ideas are:

Using phrases of the Lord's Prayer sung with symbolizing hymns.
The Affirmation of Faith punctuated with appropriate hymns.
The significant beliefs of the faith illustrated with hymns.

I. USING CHURCH SCHOOL HYMNS IN THE WORSHIP SERVICE

One idea that worked for us in a church that did not have a children's choir program was a hymn-of-the-month program.

First, a committee selected a hymn that would be appropriate for the season and for children for each month of the church year.

Next, we recruited members of the adult choir who were willing to attend a class in the children's department of the church school for the opening 10 or 15 minutes of the class session, teaching the children the selected hymn for the month. (The adults then went to their own class)

On the fourth Sunday of the month the entire children's church school sat as a body in the church service. At the appropriate time they sang the first verse of the hymn-of-the-month for the congregation. Then the entire congregation joined in singing the entire hymn. We came to this singing of the first verse only, through necessity. Our younger children who were learning the hymn by rote could only manage one verse in that length of time. We did not attempt to robe the children or process them in or out and the youngest children left the service after their singing.

We felt there were many positive aspects to this program:

1. All children were included.
2. There was not the problem of transportation or extra rehearsal time.
3. The children had the experience of singing with a large group of other children.
4. The children had the experience of leading in an aspect of congregational worship.
5. The children became acquainted with the hymnal and familiar with a number of our church hymns.

The biggest difficulty we encountered was finding meaningful hymns for such a wide age range (4-12 years old.)

LENT AND EASTER

The first event to be observed by Christians was Easter. For some time there was no general agreement upon the date of Easter. The Eastern, Roman and Gallican churches each had its own method of choosing a date. Finally, agreement was reached, about the 7th century, and now Easter occurs on the first Sunday after the full moon happening upon or next after March 21.

The season of Lent attached itself to Easter as a result of early Christian efforts to find ways of deepening the devotional approach to Easter. Lent is a 40-day period of preparation, a time of prayer and meditation.

Music belongs in this season of reflection. It can express our moods and aspirations in a way mere words cannot. It can help us and undergird us in a bold adventure of self-improvement. Music can accompany us on our journey to that great highlight and celebration of the church year—Easter.

Victories have always been announced by music—trumpets and anthems and uplifted voices—and what is Easter but the great victory celebration of our church? The loud, clear message, "He lives!" has had the power to change lives, to begin a church, to create the New Testament. We should use every resource at our command to continue to announce our victory message to the world.

This section of the book looks at a number of ways to use music in the preparation for, and the celebration of, Easter.

A. LISTENING TO MUSIC

Though by far the largest portion of this book deals with "doing" music and "making" music we must not overlook the fact that music can just *be* a pure and universal means of expressing the divine aspect of the human spirit.

A rewarding way to grow during the season of Lent is by learning to listen to great music.

We have almost lost the art of sensitive listening. Canned music is piped at us constantly in elevators, grocery stores, on our car radios. This is a good season of the year to turn inward and try to understand the meaning of the Bible passage: "Be still and know that I am God" and "The Lord is in his holy temple: Let all the earth keep silence before him." Listening should become, not a background musical experience as we go about something else, but an experience in its own right.

Begin by finding a quiet place and then just sit, still and quiet. After a while you will hear the rhythm of your pulse and heartbeat.

Next, turn on some of the beautiful music that is our heritage and especially speaks to this time of year and inward contemplation. Beethoven is appropriate, the Bach setting of the Passion, Brahm's "Requiem", Verdi's "Requiem" or your favorite composition by others of the greatest composers. Do not try to "understand" the music, accept it with your whole body, receive it fully without reservation, let it flow through you in a continual inflow and outflow of vivifying experiences.

Listening alone or with a sensitive companion is best for this experience.

Also, avail yourself of the special music concerts offered in your area and share the experience of listening to music with a family or class. There are many cantatas, oratorios and other choral music compositions written especially for Lent and Easter. Some churches have Wednesday evenings in Lent as special musical services; Maundy Thrusday is almost universally the occasion for a solemn communion service coupled with music. "Holy Week in Music" could be the theme of special Lenten observances. Profound music has a very special place in this season of soul-searching and penitence.

B. MUSIC IN THE BIBLE

Perhaps a renewed reading of the Bible is a part of your Lenten development. Let's look at the part music plays in our Bible.

Music is mentioned many times in the Bible suggesting to us its importance in the religious development of man. Some of these references seem particularly interesting and might suggest further study for your class.

I Samuel 16:14-23. The use of music by David with Saul introduces the idea of music as therapy. This is an interesting field of service today. Teenagers studying "Vocations" might like to pursue this idea by having a speaker on Musical Therapy and doing research to find out information about this field.

Matthew 26:30 Jesus and the disciples sing.

Acts 16:25 Paul and Silas sing.

Colossians 3:16-17 (especially for teachers) Teaching with song.

Look up actual songs in the Bible:
- Exodus 15:1-3 (Moses' song)
- I Samuel 2:1-10 (Hannah's song)
- II Samuel 22:2-51 (David's song)
- Luke 1:46-55 (Mary's song)

What was the context that caused these songs to be sung? Set them to original music or dance.

Here is a quiz for adults.

Many passages in the Book of Psalms refer to music. Each verse has two parts. Find the second half of each verse. Try to match column A with column B without looking up the Bible references. Check yourself by using the Bible references.

Column A

Psalm	First half of verse
33:3	Sing unto him a new song ______
40:3	He put a new song in my mouth ______
43:4	Then I will go to the altar of God, to God my exceeding joy ______
57:9	I will give thanks to thee, O Lord among the people ______
68:32	Sing to God, O kingdoms of the earth ______
69:30	I will praise the name of God with a song ______
81:2	Raise a shout, sound the timbrel ______
95:1	O come, let us sing to the Lord ______
146:2	I will praise the Lord as long as I live ______
150:4	Praise him with timbrel and dance ______
150:5	Praise him with sounding cymbals ______

Column B Second half of verse

1. play skillfully on the strings with loud shouts
2. sing praises to the Lord
3. praise him with loud clashing cymbals
4. I will magnify him with thanksgiving
5. a song of praise to our God
6. Praise him with strings and pipes
7. Let us make a joyful noise to the rock of our salvation
8. and I will praise thee with the lyre, O God, my God.
9. I will sing praises to my God while I have being
10. the sweet lyre with the harp
11. I will sing praises to thee among the nations

C. STUDY WHAT A NUMBER OF HYMNS SAY ABOUT DEATH AND ETERNAL LIFE

Easter is often a time when questions about death are raised. The old taboos seem to be lifting and people are discussing and studying the subject. As an introduction to such a study it would be interesting to look at what our hymns say about death. Following the same idea as suggested on page 27 in singing a number of hymns about Jesus, explores what our hymns are saying about death.

Using pencils and paper jot down one question or thought about death that a particular hymn raises for you. A suggested selection of hymns are:

Abide With Me
I Know Not What The Future Holds
On Jordan's Stormy Bank I Stand
For All the Saints Who From Their Labors Rest
Jerusalem the Golden
Sing With All The Sons of Glory
Rise My Soul
The Sands of Time are Sinking
Sunset and Evening Star
O Eyes That are Weary

Choose suitable hymns from your own hymnal.

Following the singing of a hymn ask each person to discuss with one other person his question or idea and what he thinks was suggested by the text.

Sing the second hymn and follow the same procedure with a different person.

When a number of hymns have been sung ask the entire group to list questions that have been raised, either from the singing or from the discussions.

List these before the group. These questions can be the basis for further research and discussion.

D. EASTER EVENTS PORTRAYED THROUGH MUSIC

Jesus Decides

Passion

Into the woods my Master went,
Clean for-spent, for-spent;
Into the woods my Master came,
For-spent with love and shame.
But the olives they were not blind to Him,
The little gray leaves were kind to Him,
The thorn tree had a mind to Him,
When into the woods He came.

Out of the woods my Master went,
And He was well content;
Out of the woods my Master came,
Content with death and shame.
When death and shame would woo Him last,
From under the trees they slew Him last,
T'was on a tree they slew Him last,
When out of the woods He came.

Words by Sidney Lanier

The singing of this lovely Lenten hymn puts before us the idea of Jesus' experience in Gethsemane. It raises questions that an individual or class should think about: Do you think Jesus could have escaped death? How? Did Jesus have a real struggle to decide what to do? What might have been the results if Jesus had escaped? Does faith in God guarantee that we will avoid trouble or pain? Does faith in God automatically guarantee that we will know how to act in all situations?

Peter and Easter

One of the most convincing evidences of the resurrection is the amazing change that happened to the disciple, Peter. It would be an interesting study to look at him "before" and "after". This lively song by Avery and Marsh, "And the Cock Begins to Crow", shows Peter before the resurrection. The authors suggest that you actually crow in this song.

After learning this song do research on Peter after the resurrection. Find evidences of the change from weak to strong, from cowardly to brave, from clumsy to skillful. Then the class might like to write their own song of Peter "after".

Questions for you to ponder and discuss:

What did the resurrection of Jesus have to do with the change in Peter?

Have you ever known anyone whose life changed through the working of the power of God? How did it happen?

AND THE COCK BEGINS TO CROW

Je---sus told him:"Pe-ter, you'll de-
had an op---por--tu--ni---ty to
needs you ve---ry bad--ly stand---ing
cause it's not a bet-ter place to

ny me"? Poor, poor Pete! His face got
show him. Poor, poor Pete! But then to
by him. Just like Pete! But you re-
live in. We're like Pete! We'd be like

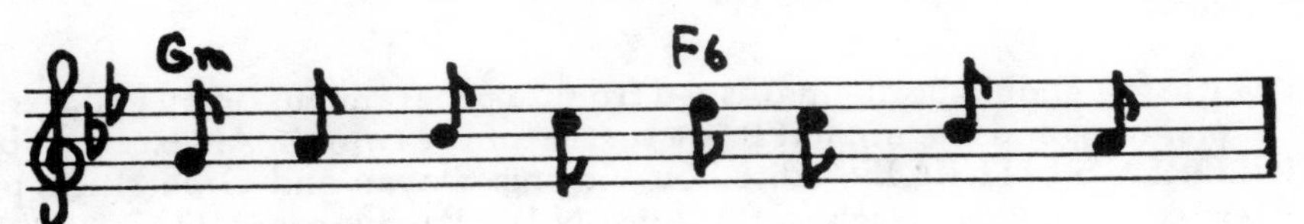

red and he got ang-ry and he
peo-ple who kept ask-ing:"Aren't you
fuse to stand by him it's just like
Pe--ter if in-stead of say---ing

shout---ed: "No, I won't, my Lord, just
one of them?" he an-swered:"I don't
Pe-----ter and the Lord cause you de--
"Right, and I must change it!" we would

try me!" Poor, poor Peter! And the
know him!"
--ny him.
give in.

Palm Sunday

Palm Sunday marks the entry of Jesus into Jerusalem and the beginning of the dramatic last week of his life. Special music usually accompanies this day. "ST. MATTHEW PASSION" is often sung in church services as is "THE PALMS" by Jean-Baptiste Faure. "Hosanna, Laud Hosanna, the Little Children Sang" is a favorite hymn as well as "Ride on! Ride on in Majesty".

In your church school class you might learn one of these hymns or use the third verse of "Tell Me the Stories of Jesus (which tell of the children entering Jerusalem, waving palm branches and singing "Hosannas").

This is a good hymn to accompany with movement and the waving of palm branches. Then the class could draw a large mural of the palm Sunday scene, each student drawing a picture of himself in the crowd waving branches and rejoicing.

E. MUSIC IN CHILDREN'S LITURGY

"Children's Liturgy" is a term used to refer to a service of the church geared particularly to children. It recognizes that children belong in our worshipping assemblies and that children learn about God, not just through formal instruction, but also by experiencing his presence in worship. They, as well as adults, need the opportunity to come to church to give their thanks. Since it is a child-oriented service it will have the color, movement and participation to which children respond. Music for these liturgies should also be totally involving. It should be music to which children (and adults) can move and clap and participate and respond. There should be freedom to use instruments and move rhythmically in these services.

"Children's Liturgy" should be distinguished from "a program put on by children". Children take the leadership in planning and leading but it is a service of the church. An excellent book for study in this area is CHILDREN'S LITURGIES edited by Virginia Sloyan and Gabe Huck, published by The Liturgical Conference, 1330 Massachusetts Ave. N.W. Washington, D.C. 20005. Also SIGNS, STORIES AND SONG, Virginia Sloyan, editor (same address).

Palm Sunday with its Biblical tradition of children and movement and color would be a good time for a Children's Liturgy.

Some ways to use music in such a service are:

1. A procession of children, single or double file marching in rhythm, waving palm branches and singing.
2. A long follow-the-leader line of children and adults singing "Lord of the Dance."
3. Have everyone bring a rhythm instrument to the service and play along as they sing, "Hosanna, Laud Hosanna, the Little Children Sing."
4. Do rhythmic movement to the spiritual "Lonesome Valley".
5. Sing the spiritual "Let Us Cheer the Weary Traveler". Let a leader sing the refrain while everyone hums. All join in the chorus.
6. Sing the folk song, "What Wondrous Love is This?" with accompaniment on tambourines, triangles and finger-cymbals.

F. TRUMPET SOUNDS

The majesty and dignity of trumpets or a brass chorus add an unforgettable intensity to the color and sound of the Easter celebration.

To prepare your class for this experience study together Numbers 10:1-10, particularly verse 10: "On the day of your gladness also and at your appointed feasts and at the beginnings of your months you shall blow the trumpets over your burnt offerings; they shall serve you for remembrance before your God; I am the Lord your God."

Also read Joel 2:1:

"Blow the trumpet in Zion; sound the alarm on my holy mountain. Let all the inhabitants of the land tremble for the day of the Lord is coming, it is near."

For class or individual research, work may be done on the use of trumpets in Old Testament times. How did they look? What was their function? How has their use in religious celebrations changed? THE ILLUSTRATED WORLD OF THE BIBLE LIBRARY SERIES McGraw-Hill, Publishers is a good resource here. Also EVERYDAY LIFE IN BIBLE TIMES published by the National Geographic Society and BIBLE ENCYCLOPEDIA FOR CHILDREN, Cecil Northcott, Westminster Press has some information.

In addition, it is interesting to study the Easter morning celebration which is held in Bethlehem, Pennsylvania. This was one of the first Easter services to be held in our country and is continued to the present day. The service always begins with a trombone chorus blaring joyfully forth at 3:00 on Easter morning. Though it is still dark the people gather at the Old Moravian Burying Ground near the church and await the rising of the sun. When the sun appears, the trombone choir blares forth again and the thousands of voices join in singing, "Christ is risen!"

Can your class or an individual member find other examples of the use of trumpets and other brass to celebrate Easter? Perhaps they are used in sunrise services near your home.

G. EASTER BELLS

This is a good song to use with 6 tonal blocks. Strike the blocks on "Ding! Dong! Ding! Dong! they say" and on "Ding! Dong! It's Easter Day."

E G E G A D E G G A B C

Reprinted by permission

H. HYMNS FOR EASTERTIDE

Empty and barren would be our services of worship today without the congregational singing of hymns. Many powerful hymns have been written to celebrate the Easter season. Since Eastertide includes the 40 days between Resurrection and Ascension, it is possible to include a number of these Easter hymns in your celebration.

One church began their celebration of the Sunday following Easter Sunday with "Music for Worship and Praise". They followed this format:

"Low in the Grave He Lay" (stanzas 1,3)
(sopranos in the congregation sang the verses and the entire congregation sang the chorus)

"Come Ye Faithful, Raise the Strain"
(entire congregation sang stanzas 1,5. The minister read the other three stanzas)

Old Testament Lesson Job 19:1,21-27

"I Know that my Redeemer Lives"
(entire congregation sang entire hymn)

New Testament Lesson 1 Cor. 15:12-22

"Ask Ye What Great Things I Know"
(choir asked questions, congregation responds)

Piano and Organ alternated as accompaniment.

Many groups today are finding added meaning in sharing the musical responses and singing the hymns in new, creative ways, not merely using them as opportunities to stand up and stretch. Hymns should have a carefully planned purpose in worship and should synchronize with the entire service.

New hymns should be a frequent part of the worship celebration, but it seems to be true of human nature that we shy away from trying new hymns. If you ask a person, "What is a good hymn?" the answer usually boils down to, "The ones I know". The methods suggested above; singing a part of the hymn, reading the words of a new hymn, listening carefully to the music, etc. may ease the unfamiliarity of a new hymn and help us extend our musical and spiritual horizons into something new.

I. MAKE WIND CHIMES

Easter brings the message of God's goodness and love and we also see signs of that love in the coming of Spring. It is therefore appropriate at this time of year to celebrate Spring with its wonders and beauty.

Bring the music of Spring into your home or classroom by making wind chimes. For this project you will need:

disposable plastic glasses (several for each chime)
an oven
a hammer
a dowel stick (one for each chime)
clear fishing line
foil covered cookie sheet

Give each person several disposable plastic glasses. They come in a variety of colors. Turn each glass upside down and tap the bottoms gently with a hammer to produce cracks. Be careful not to smash or break! Place the cracked glasses several inches apart and upside down on a foil-covered cookie sheet. Place the sheet in a 350 degree oven. If you have a glass door on your oven the fun is increased because you can watch the glasses gradually collapse and form interesting ring shapes. When all have collapsed remove from the oven and allow to cool. Perhaps while they are cooling the next person's cookie sheet can go into the oven and the fun of watching begins again.

When the rings are cool enough to handle, tie them with the fishing line to the dowel stick. They should hang at varying levels but close enough together to touch each other and create sounds as the wind blows. The wind chimes may be hung from a tree or on a porch.

J. SPRING SONGS

There are many songs of Spring's awakening in our curriculum material and in song books from the library. This is one of the favorite of the young children at Walker Chapel United Methodist Church in Arlington, Virginia. It was written by the mother of a church member.

For several Sundays in March while we look for songs of Spring and wait and hope for the gentle weather to begin we sing this song. Of course, all the children "ruffle their feathers" in imitation of the robin as they sing.

THE ROBIN IN MARCH

Words and Music
by Ruth Stephens Porter

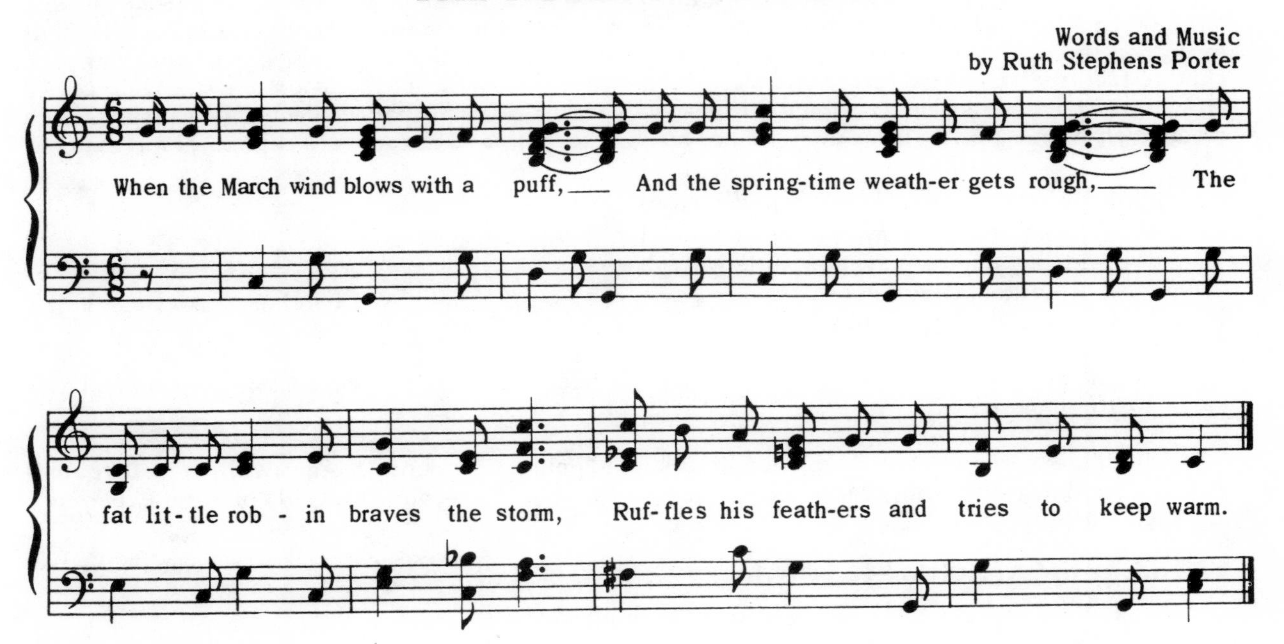

Reprinted by permission

PENTECOST

Pentecost comes 50 days after Easter and is considered the birthday of the Church. In the early church, Pentecost ranked with Christmas and Easter as the third great festival of the Christian year. It was considered one of the happiest times of the Church calendar, celebrated with songs and feasting.

Today, Pentecost is a time of rejuvenation and revitalization. It celebrates the coming of the Holy Spirit and this period (stretching to Advent in some churches—roughly half of the year) celebrates the beginning and ongoing life of the church.

The symbols of this season are flames of fire and rushing winds. These symbols inspire expression of movements that are free and creative. They suggest the use of a variety of sounds. So, in this section of the book we look at the use of rhythmic movements and the creative use of instruments. This section looks at how early Christians sang and includes songs appropriate for this season.

For convenience we have also included here a look at instruments used in the church and church school. We will look at which ones to buy and how they can be used, and a general look at the use of rhythmic movement in the classroom. Considerations that are appropriate for all year, not just for Pentecost.

A. RHYTHMIC MOVEMENT

Rhythmic movement is an art form. It is an ability to use the body to rhythmically express feelings and ideas. It capitalizes on many positive aspects of children: their imagination, their love of movement and their eagerness to try and to do.

Some rhythmic movement can be a group expression (as in the movement to "In Christ There is No East or West"). Look at rhythmic movement now as an individual activity where each student examines and expresses his own ideas. Rhythmic activities should provide the opportunity for each child to feel free and self-directed and also give a means for outward expression of inner feelings. All students can achieve success on their various levels and enjoy participation. Each child's response in a creative rhythmic activity is his own. He has his own feelings and purposes to express or not express.

What do you need for these activities?

1. Space. Either a multipurpose room or fellowship hall or outdoor space.
2. Piano, record player or tape recorder.
3. Rhythm instruments
4. Loose-fitting, comfortable clothes. No shoes. (Heavy shoes hamper movement)

The teacher sets the mood for the activity. His/Her enthusiasm and freedom to move will give value to the experience.

The first experience of rhythmic activities should help the student become aware of his/her abilities. It should help the student lose self-consciousness about movement and help him/her experience joy through movement.

Warming up Activities to Music

1. Skip around the room without touching anyone.
2. Make the smallest shape you can.
3. Make the shape of a circle.
4. Move in a slow, steady way. Be something growing.
5. Show by movements that you are very, very heavy, like an elephant.
6. Show by movements that you are very light, like a balloon.
7. How high can you go? Can you move from very low to very high?

These warming up activities and others you can suggest challenge each child to explore and discover his capacities for movement. You might talk with the group here about how each person walks or runs differently and how the way we move often expresses the way we feel. After the students are comfortable with moving suggest activities that involve moods.

1. How do you move when you are happy?
2. How do you move when you are tired?
3. If you were very frightened, how would you move?
4. How do you move when you are angry? (Hard, aggressive movements should not be avoided. They can provide a release of tension, as long as students do not touch each other)

As the student learns by exploration how he can move his body he is increasing his vocabulary of skills that can help him to express ideas, moods, music, and experiences. You have used the love of movement for its own sake. Now you are ready to use movement to:

express and communicate,
to music,
to Bible stories. . . . .

Moving To Music

The first experience of movement to music may best be done with a short instrumental recording such as a selection from "Carnival of the Animals" by Saint-Säens or from "The Nutcracker Suite" by Tschaikovsky or "Golliwog's Cakewalk" by Debussy. Have students listen to the music. They may close their eyes, clap the rhythm, find the flow of the beat with their arms.

Next, the teacher should talk with the students about the music—the story it tells or what it is about. The students can share ideas about how the music makes them feel.

You might bring a folk tune with words for the class to listen to and interpret with movement. "Blowin' in the Wind" with words and music by Bob Dylan is especially appropriate for the season of Pentecost. Again the emphasis is on individual interpretation. Listen to the music and words, talk about what it is saying, try to feel the swaying rhythm, then move as the song inspires you. Teenagers especially enjoy moving to this song.

The next step might be to work as a group to interpret hymns and songs. The books by Margaret Fisk Taylor are excellent resources for getting you started in this direction. (TIME FOR WONDER AND TIME FOR DISCOVERY, United Church Press).

Moving To Bible Stories

The rhythm or mood of stories can be expressed through movement. Rhythm instruments can be used for accompaniment and to set a rhythmic feeling. For example:

The Creation of the Animals

When the world was new it was covered with a lush greenness. Seeds were scattered upon the earth and the seeds grew and grew and grew and expanded and expanded and expanded.

(pause for seeds to grow. The shaking of a tambourine is a good accompaniment for this.)

And there was water on the face of the earth—seas and rivers and oceans, and the waves flowed and swayed.

(pause for motions. Xylophone accompaniment perhaps)

And from the waters came forth living creatures, great whales and huge sea fish.

(pause for fish)

Then the birds appeared. All kinds, all sizes, flapping and swooping and gliding.

(pause for birds)

And God blessed them saying: Be fruitful and multiply and fill the waters in the seas and let fowl multiply over the earth.

(pause for action)

Next, came the creatures from the earth—cattle and creeping things and beasts of the earth—running and slinking and plodding and stalking.

(pause for animals)

And the variety and beauty and grace of movement of these animals was unbelievable. They covered the earth.
(pause for action)

The story of Noah and the ark can be done in a similar fashion to the story above. Try to use words that suggest movement.

The beautiful rhythmic interpretation for an older group would be to use the story of God talking to Job about the animals in Job 39:5-8, 19-29. "Hast thou given the horse strength? He paweth in the valley and rejoiceth in his strength. . .". Verses such as these can come alive with a sensitive, creative group.

How can a teacher make use of rhythmic movement? Many churches allow children to leave the worship service during the sermon and latter portion of the service for an instructive activity on their age level. This would be a good time for first experiences in rhythmic movement, led by someone experienced in the field. After children have had experience with warming-up activities and moving to music and stories they should feel comfortable enough to use it in their classrooms. A teacher could assign a group to interpret a Bible selection using only a small amount of time or an entire session could be used working out the rhythmic movements to a hymn. The selection could be used in a traditional class setting or as a learning center assignment.

B. RHYTHMIC MOVEMENT USING SCARVES OR STREAMERS

The use of scarves or streamers can add another dimension to your rhythmic movement.

Step 1: Read together Acts 2:1-4
"When the day of Pentecost had come they were all together in one place. And suddenly a sound came from heaven like the rush of a mighty wind, and it filled all the house where they were sitting. And there appeared to them tongues as of fire, distributed and resting on each one of them. And they were all filled with the Holy Spirit and began to speak in other tongues, as the Spirit gave them utterance."

Step 2: Look at pictures of some of the symbols associated with the season of Pentecost: the flame, the dove, and the wind. Perhaps the class can suggest others.

Step 3: Working as a group, write a simple explanation of each symbol. For example: "I am a flame. This fire will never burn out because it is a reminder of the power of God in our lives." I am the Wind. I am moving and blowing and swirling. I am unseen but powerful like the Spirit of God in our lives."

Step 4: Have colored scarves or paper streamers for each student. As the teacher reads the explanation of each symbol let the class move rhythmically, swirling with red and orange streamers or scarves for the flame, blue streamers or scarves for the wind, white streamers or scarves for the dove. Accompaniment can be drums or tambourines.

C. HANDS AS INSTRUMENTS

What would the world be without rhythm? "God made the world and he gave to it a meter, a beat, a tempo and a rhythm."

This rhythm can set out hands clapping and our feet tapping. Sometimes our church music lacks a joyful quality. A certain feeling of enthusiasm, vitality or exuberance is missing. The human voice is basically legato or smooth. An eternal legato does not create joyful feelings. But turn a class loose, clapping hands or tapping feet or snapping fingers and immediately excitement and vitality spring forth.

"Every Time I Feel the Spirit" is a good clapping song.

Other hand movements, in addition to clapping hands and snapping fingers can be used to enliven songs. You can pat your knees, hit one fist on top of another, pound one fist into the opposite palm, touch elbows in rhythm.

Use fingers as drumsticks and the desk or table as drum and roll fingers in order, or, tap each finger separately, or, use combination of:

roll-tap-tap
roll-tap-tap
roll, roll, roll, tap-tap

If you have limited space but need pep and enthusiasm in your singing, finger snapping and rhythmic hand and arm movements can solve your problem.

D. RHYTHM INSTRUMENTS

Students can easily transfer their basic responses to music. Clapping hands and tapping feet to rhythm instruments can be handled skillfully. The use of these instruments greatly widens the potentialities of happy and creative participation in music. It is comforting to many teachers to know that you do not have to be a professional musician or even a talented one in order to guide students in the use of rhythm instruments. You should be at ease and willing to try new things and experiment with sounds.

Playing of musical instruments has been acknowledged as part of our religious heritage from the beginning of the Hebrew record in Genesis. Your class might be interested in becoming a part of this history.

PSALM 100

Step 1: Let the class experiment with a number of rhythm instruments, getting the feel and sounds the different instruments make. Let the student choose the instrument he wants.

Step 2: Read Psalm 100 with an exaggerated marching rhythm. Let the students beat the rhythm with you on their instruments.

Step 3: Students, with their instruments, form a procession of people going to the Temple. They can sing and chant the Psalm with you as they play and march.

Rhythm instruments can be used in other processionals. "Now Thank We All Our God" is a good hymn to use as children march, each playing his/her own instrument.

All instruments do not have to be used every time. One or two instruments can be used with songs for rhythmic emphasis. They can be used to add sound effects to a Bible or curriculum story. For example, woodblocks, sticks and sand blocks can be used to imitate the sound of builders, repairmen and other workmen. Rattles can be falling rain, etc. Rhythm instruments can also be accompaniment to rhythmic movement. There are many possibilities for the creative use of these instruments. Be adventuresome!

Rhythm instruments do not need to be restricted solely to children. One of the most joyful musical evenings I remember was one in which a group of senior citizens performed on homemade rhythm instruments featuring a washtub bass.

Some guides in buying rhythm instruments:

1. Triangles should have a ringing, bell-like tone. High pitched ones with a small striker produce a gentle ring.
2. A clear sounding cymbal is better than several with dull, thudding tones.
3. Tambourines should have a soft, shimmering quality to the jingles, not harsh and tinny.
4. Wood blocks should make a snappy sound.

5. You will need one or more sturdy bongo drums
6. A basic list of rhythm instruments includes:

   sticks, claves, wood blocks, tone blocks, sand blocks, castanets, for wooden sounds.

   bells and triangles are needed for more resonant effects.

   drums, cymbals, tambourines, tom-toms, maracas and jingle clogs provide the heavier tones.

   novelty instruments such as bird whistles, ratchets and rhythm tone gourds.

If you are making your own instruments:

"Imagination" is the key word here. Large juice cans, coffee cans, kegs and round cereal boxes can become drums and tom-toms. Drumheads can be rubber, heavy fabric, oilcloth or skin. Or you can just turn a big metal wastebasket upside down and use it for a drum.

Dowels make good sticks. They can become jingle sticks by fastening bells, bottle caps or metal washers to them.

Blocks of wood covered with sandpaper are simple-to-make sandblocks.

Paper plates with bottle caps attached to add a jingling sound to make tambourines.

Jars containing pebbles can make effective maracas.

Two metal pie tins and two large drawer knobs make cymbals or use pan tops hit with a spoon.

The tops from tin cans can be hung on a stick and used as jangles.

Dry beans can be placed in a can and shaken.

WORSHIP

NUN DANKET. 6.7.6.7.6.6.6.6.
MARTIN RINKART, 1586–1649
Tr. by CATHERINE WINKWORTH, 1829–1878
JOHANN CRÜGER, 1598–1662
Harmonized by
FELIX MENDELSSOHN-BARTHOLDY, 1809–1847
1. Now thank we all our God With heart and hands and voic - es,
2. O may this boun - teous God, Through all our life be near us,
3. All praise and thanks to God The Fa - ther now be giv - en,
Who won - drous things hath done, In whom His world re - joic - es;
With ev - er joy - ful hearts And bless - ed peace to cheer us;
The Son, and Him who reigns With them in high - est heav - en,
Who, from our moth - ers' arms, Hath blessed us on our way
And keep us in His grace, And guide us when per - plexed,
The one e - ter - nal God, Whom earth and heaven a - dore;
With count - less gifts of love, And still is ours to - day.
And free us from all ills In this world and the next.
For thus it was, is now, And shall be ev - er - more. A-MEN.

E. TAMBOURINES AND FINGER CYMBALS

Technically classed as rhythm instruments, tambourines and finger cymbals can be used in more sophisticated musical experiences. The tambourine is one of the most versatile percussion instruments. It may be rattled or struck sharply with all the fingers, with the knuckles or with the heel of the hand. You can buy tambourines with or without a drum head or skin.

Finger cymbals can be bought at music stores, but for unusual sounding antique finger cymbals your best bet is often import houses or church members who have collected cymbals in their travels.

The use of tambourine, finger cymbals and triangle adds a joyful percussion sound to many songs. These are effective instruments to use with teenagers.

As in the use of all rhythm instruments, be creative for the most joyful and happy sounds. Your purpose in using these instruments is to add zest and verve to your music.

F. JUBAL'S INSTRUMENTS

In Genesis 4:21 music is first mentioned in the Bible. "His brother's name was Jubal, he was the father of all those who play the lyre and pipe."

Our precedent for the use of varied and expressive musical instruments goes back a long way to Moses, Miriam, and David. You're in good company when you use musical instruments to express your joys and longings to God.

In addition to rhythm instruments what others can we use in our church school and congregational worship?

The organ probably springs first to your mind as *the* established instrument for use in churches. It is an interesting note to insert here that, at one time, the organ was considered "the devil's bagpipes". It was far too innovative and worldly to be included in a service of worship, some people thought. Some of the very same arguments we hear today concerning the use of electronic or contemporary music were once addressed as objections to the organ.

The second most common instrument in our churches is the piano. It is standard equipment in many classrooms. Unfortunately it is frequently in poor repair and out of tune. The piano needs attention as a teaching tool and as an investment. There should be regular tuning (at least once a year) and a minimum temperature of 66°F in cold weather. If you are buying a piano consider also the new electronic pianos. Though only five octaves, these pianos have many advantages for church schools:

1. They are about half the price of a regular piano.
2. They take up less space.
3. They do not go out of tune.
4. They come equipped with ear phones, which is a decided advantage in open classroom/learning centers.
5. They are portable.

Do not confuse electronic pianos with home organs! There is a big difference. The four leading manufacturers of electronic pianos are:

1. Wurlitzer 2. Baldwin 3. Rhodes 4. Electrokey

No matter what make or model is selected the electronic piano is ideal for classroom use. Your local music store should be able to tell you what is available in your area. Remember, the purpose is classroom use rather than a vehicle for performance.

The autoharp is another good instrument for church school use. Few musical experiences bring personal satisfaction as quickly and as easily as playing the autoharp. Children can master it after a few rehearsal hours. Its chief use would be to accompany small group singing whenever a keyboard instrument is not available. Many of the songs in curriculum material include chords for autoharp. A pamphlet, "ENJOY PLAYING THE AUTOHARP" by Irvin Wolfe is available from Discipleship Resources P.O. Box 840 Nashville, Tenn. 37202, for 15 cents a copy or twelve copies for $1.50. It contains instructions for playing and tuning the autoharp.

One of my favorite instruments is tonal bells or resonator bells. These are metal bars attached to blocks of wood. When struck with a hammer the bars produce an unusually lovely sound. One advantage is that each block is separate. A child may be given one or more. They are accurately tuned to the diatonic scale and are constructed in such a way that it is almost impossible for them to get out of tune. A beginner set of 8 bells can be bought for about $15. There are also sets for 20 bells and 25 bells.

I find these bells better than small marimbas or xylophones because they have a larger striking surface and may be used by the entire class at the same time. In using these bells with first graders I have them sit in a semi-circle facing me, the teacher. On each child's lap is a hymn book and the bell rests on the book to steady it. I point to each child when it is time for his/her bell to strike. They were able to accompany themselves to "Kum Ba Yah" after only one run-through of the song.

KUM BA YAH for tonal bells (6 bells)

C E GGG
A A G
C E GGG
F E D
C E GGG
A A G
F E C
D D C

A number of simple song instructions come with the bells. We quickly learned "Twinkle, Twinkle Little Star" and then wrote our own words to accompany the lesson for the day. Thanks to Laura Ostrom and her first and second grade class for these words to the tune of Twinkle, Twinkle Little Star":

Jesus was so kind and true
Helping friends like me and you.
He helped both the sick and poor
Showed them with his loving ways
How to live as God's own child
Ever loving, gentle, mild.

and they added a coda:

Whether you are big or small
Jesus loves you one and all.

Handbells, though expensive and requiring a trained director, are very effective instruments to provide a new and different tone color to a worship service. Ways they can be used in a formal service of worship are:

Prelude
Ringing of the hour
Processional by handbell choir
Prelude to or ringing with congregational singing
Accompaniment for certain anthems
Handbell offertory
Postlude.

Guitars are a popular instrument for accompaniment in both church school and worship. Invite these and other instrumentalists in the church to visit the class one Sunday and accompany the students' singing. Young musicians would welcome the experience and older people might be encouraged to retrieve an old violin or clarinet from their closets at home. Zithers and dulcimers are also possible accompaniment instruments. Community resources may make available instruments of foreign origin and cultures.

The range of Jubal's instruments is as wide as your experience and imagination. Glass containers (the thinner the better) can be tuned by pouring water into them to make a set of glass chimes. Play the glasses with spoons. Pieces of sheet metal (with the edges taped for safety) can be shaken to produce thunder or ceremonial gongs.

Even photographs and tape recorders can be utilized as instruments. And an overhead projector is useful in teaching new songs.

Any instrument that adds vigor and vitality to our music and to our worship of God is surely one of Jubal's instruments.

G. VISIT AN ORGAN

It is an exciting experience to take your class to visit a pipe-organ (either in your own or a neighboring church). Try to arrange not only to see the console, but to get in among the pipes. The church organist might be willing to explain the workings of the organ to your class as well as give a demonstration and perhaps even let the students try out the organ.

Theodore Ripper, writing about the pipe organ in MUSIC MINISTRY (Sept. 1973 issue) made an interesting comparison between the parts of an organ and the groupings of mankind. He said: "A *pipe* is to the organ as a *person* is to mankind. A *rank* or *stop* is to the organ as a *family* is to mankind. *Similar sounding ranks* are to the organ as *ethnic groupings* are to mankind. *Combinations of stops* are to the organ as *organizations* or *groups* are to mankind. *Full organ* is to the organ as the *total community* is to mankind."

Ask your church organist to use this comparison when explaining the organ to older children and youth. This seems a fascinating way to illustrate brotherhood and world community as well as learn about the organ. "Hearing" the illustration adds an exciting new dimension to the learning. After the visit ask the class to illustrate this concept.

This is also a good time for students to sit in the choir loft and sing a hymn they have learned, guided by the organist.

H. HOW DID THE FIRST CHRISTIANS SING?

As we think together during the season of the year about the beginning of the Christian Church it is interesting to speculate how the first Christians sang because we read from the Epistles of Paul that they had "Psalms and hymns and spiritual songs" whenever they met together.

More than likely this singing was a form of chanting in which long sentences were sung on one note with occasional embellishments for the important words. Most of the texts were probably from the Book of Psalms, where the vivid language helped to transform spoken words into sung phrases. The "Gloria Patri" has been identified as an early church song which might have been sung by worshipping Christians.

The Christians in Rome met secretly in the dark catacombs under the city holding services by candlelight and using the tombs of their saints for altars. The murmured chanting of psalms must have echoed mysteriously through the network of narrow passages.

It would be a moving experience for your class to recreate this event from our distant past. A section called "In the Catacombs" from the kit WHEN WE WERE FIRST CALLED CHRISTIANS by Judy Smith, (Contemporary Drama Service, Box 457 Downers Grove, Ill,) gives instructions for creating an environment simulating early Christian times. Directions are given for using boxes to create a life-size replica of the narrow corridors of the catacombs, with memorials and symbols on the walls, the smell of fresh, damp earth, the flicker of candles. If your church contains a long, windowless corridor that is not in use this might also be transformed into catacombs by the use of brown wrapping paper on the walls and drawn-on symbols and slabs for tombs. Encyclopedias and books on church history give information on these underground burial places.

The long, narrow corridors in the catacombs wind in a subterranean maze opening to a number of small rooms containing small altars. Here the early Christians met for their worship service.

Create a small room at the end of your corridor and simulate an early worship experience. You might include the Lord's Supper which was an important liturgy in these early services. You might include the Lord's Prayer which the early Christians probably knew.

For the singing choose a favorite Psalm. The verses of the Psalms are nearly always divided into halves, each half expressing the same idea in a different way. "O come let us sing unto the Lord: Let us make a joyful noise to the rock of our salvation". Practice chanting a verse on one level of pitch, with the free rhythm of the spoken word. Let the voice rise at the end of the first half and fall at the end of the second half in a question/answer style. This keeps the listeners' interest alive and helps to make the meaning clear.

It is an interesting fact that from the simple recitation of Psalms such as you will experience with your class, chanting developed into extended lines of free, flowing melody. In the sixth century Pope Gregory collected all the existing chants, hundreds of which had been invented by early worshippers and arranged them in the order in which they are still sung every Sunday and Saints Day in many churches and cathedrals throughout the Roman Catholic world.

It might make an interesting culmination of your study to visit one of these services.

I. YOUTH AND MUSIC

It is interesting to note how many of the folk-type songs, loved by teenagers particularly, use symbols that we associate with the season of Pentecost:

"Blowin' in the Wind"
"It only takes a spark to get the fire going"
"We are one in the Spirit"

Teenage music is in a constant state of flux and what is popular today may be out of date tomorrow. Yet these symbols of Pentecost with their urgency and intensity keep recurring.

To keep abreast of current songs for today's young people there is a helpful publication: MUSIC AND THE YOUNG, P.O. Box 840, Nashville, Tenn. 37202. This sheet, appearing 11 times a year, looks at the most popular songs, trends in music, current singers. It suggests helpful ways to understand and interpret what the songs are saying.

Accepting the fact that music is a reflection of society and popular songs can give us an idea of where youth are today, many youth groups have helpful programs in which youth bring their favorite records and the group discusses what the records are saying. Sometimes verbal analysis of the songs by theologians and psychologists are given. A danger to be aware of in this kind of verbal analysis of popular ballads is that we read more into the song than is actually there. It is doubtful that many of the popular songs are all that theological.

What about the surge of contemporary youth services of worship?

Many young people are involved in creating new forms of worship or celebration. The market currently is flooded with contemporary youth services—folk masses, rock musicals. They range all the way from very good to very bad. An important question to keep before us as we consider this form of music is: "Can it be used in reverence and sincerity without a deliberate attempt to shock?" Dancing, hand clapping, rock music, humor are not irreverent per se. But in a church service they must always contribute to the creation of the spirit of worship.

There are several positive considerations:

1. Young people are involved in active participation in worship.
2. It gives the congregation an opportunity to hear youth-oriented music.
3. It brings a sense of joyousness, vitality and celebration into the service of worship.

J. WE ARE THE CHURCH—HOW DO YOU TEACH THIS SONG?

A great song for the season of Pentecost and the beginning of the church is "We Are The Church" by Richard Avery and Donald Marsh. This song is loved by all ages. Here is one suggestion for teaching it to young children.

If you hear a story for a number of times it becomes boring but, the more familiar you are with a song the better you like it. This is a good principle to remember in teaching a song. Do not just hand your class a new song cold, and expect them to sing it the first time, but break it down into small sections until it becomes familiar.

Step 1: On the piano play the melody line of the first phrase.

Step 2: Ask the students to clap this rhythm with you.

Step 3: Now ask the children to listen and see how many times they hear that rhythm as you play the first three measures.

Step 4: Praise them when they correctly say "three".

Step 5: Tell them the words to the first three measures: "I am the church" (point to yourself) "You are the church" (point to them) "We are the church together" (include the whole group in your motion)

Step 6: Sing this much of the song with them.

Step 7: Tell them the next set of words, "All who follow Jesus, All around the world, Yes, we're the church together.

Step 8: Shape the first phrase of this melody with your hand in the air.

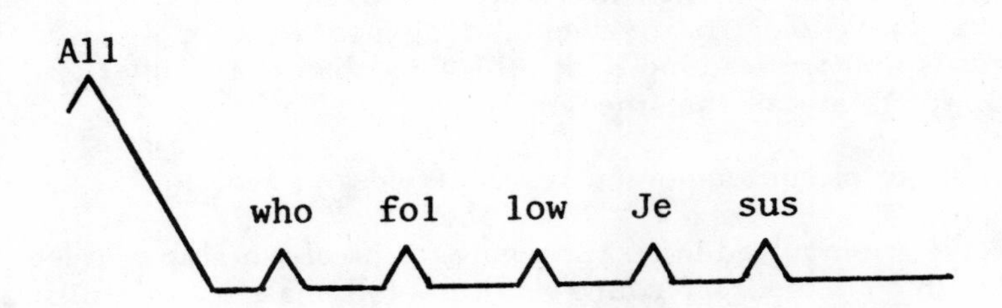

Step 9: Shape the second phrase one space higher.

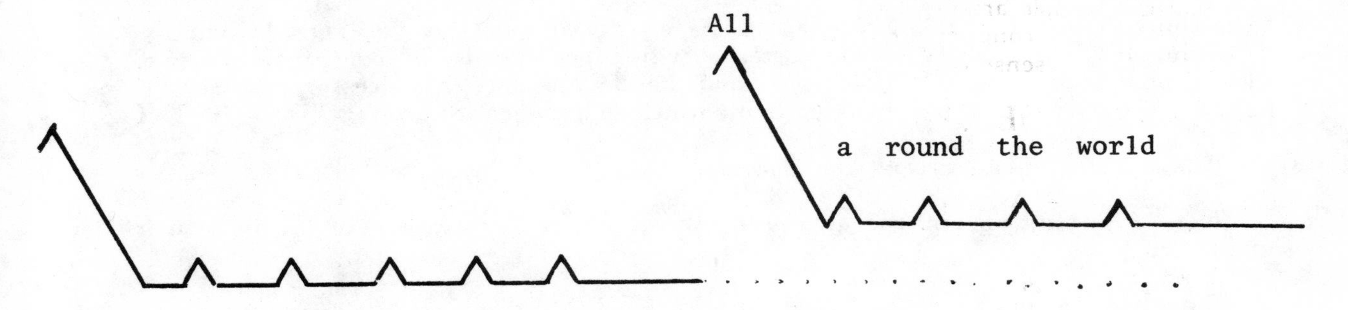

Step 10: Explain that there are only two notes in each phrase. Have them shape in the air and sing with you.

Now take the same notes one note higher.
Shape the third phrase for them.

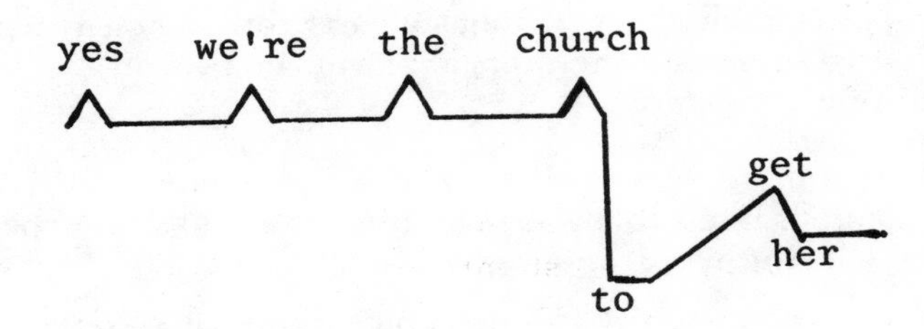

Step 11: Have them shape and sing this phrase with you.

Step 12: Play these three phrases on the piano as they sing with you.

Step 13: Now put the first and second part of the song together. You have learned the chorus.

With very young children I would stop here. At the next session they can repeat what they have learned and can learn the verse. With other children I would continue in this manner:

Step 14: Ask the class to listen to the skipping melody that goes with the words, "The church is not a building."

Step 15: Have them sing this with you.

Step 16: Explain that the next phrase uses the same skipping melody one note higher to the words, "The church is not a steeple".

Step 17: Have them sing this phrase with you.

Step 18: Going still another note higher we continue the same skipping rhythm to the words, "The church is not a resting place".

Step 19: Have them sing it with you.

Step 20: Play and sing for them with exaggerated dramatics, the words, "The church is a people".

Step 21: Sing this much of the song with them: "The church is not a building"; call out (up a note): "The church is not a steeple" (up a note); The church is not a resting place. The church is a people".

Step 22: Now, swing into the already familiar chorus, "I am the church", etc.

If you are teaching the song by rote, stop here. At the next session review their learning in this manner:

"The church is not a what?"	(make a box shape with your hand suggesting a building)
"The church is not a what?"	(make a steeple with cupped hands and pointed forefingers)
"The church is not a what?"	(fold your hands beside your face in a sleeping position)
"The *is* what?"	(make a motion including the entire group)

The students are to call out the answers.

Now, if the students can read, give out the words to the other six verses or display them in front of the group.

Teaching a song:

There are many ways to teach a song that make it more interesting and more quickly grasped. We have mentioned a few:

1. Have the students clap the rhythm
2. Have them listen for repeated phrases.
3. Shape the melody in the air (this helps them visualize when notes go up and down.)
4. Use motions to illustrate words.

The most widely used method of teaching songs by rote to non-readers is the simple approach of asking the group first to listen and then repeat as you sing a short section of the song. Some other suggestions for teaching songs are:

5. Check that your students are really reading the music by playing a few notes of the song on the piano as they follow along. Stop the music unexpectedly and have the group quickly speak the word under the last note played.
6. Give students opportunity to sing alone. "Who will solo the first line?" Younger children especially enjoy this and it creates a spontaneous, unaffected attitude toward singing.
7. Give students opportunity to set simple poems or Bible verses to their own original melody. What can they do with "I will sing with the Spirit and I will sing with understanding also?" I Cor. 14:15.
8. Give students opportunity to create their own rhythmic patterns to songs you are learning. Bongo drums are good for this.
9. Have listening games. Play a short phrase of a song. Ask students: Are notes repeated? Do they go higher or lower? Play a note on the piano and have students match it with their voices. Have students stand up when they hear the highest note in the tune.
10. Using a blackboard and chalk have students draw a line picture of the melody.

Occasionally the classroom teacher feels totally inadequate to teach a new hymn or song. In this case teach from a tape-recorder phrase by phrase. A record can also be used but a tape-recorder is easier as you can stop and start where you wish.

WE ARE THE CHURCH

2. We're many kinds of people
   With many kinds of faces,
   All colors and all ages, too from
   All times and places. *(Chorus)*

3. Sometimes the church is marching
   Sometimes it's bravely burning,
   Sometimes it's riding, sometimes hiding,
   Always it's learning: *(Chorus)*

4. And when the people gather
   There's singing and there's praying,
   There's laughing and there's crying sometimes,
   All of it saying: *(Chorus)*

5. At Pentecost some people
   Received the Holy Spirit
   And told the Good News thru the world to
   All who would hear it. *(Chorus)*

6. I Count if I am 90,
   Or 9 or just a baby;
   There's one thing I am sure about, and
   I don't mean maybe: *(Chorus)*

Sing the song, and DO the song---using gestures and movement with a different partner on each chorus.

"I am the church"---with your thumb, point to yourself.

"You are the church"---point to your partner.

"We are the church"---shake hands.

"All who follow Jesus"---circle arms over head.

"Yes, we're the church together"---link arms.

Then sing the next verse.

GOD THE CREATOR

In the season from the end of Pentecost to the beginning of Advent we find the least consistency. In some churches Pentecost extends to Advent. In some churches there is a season between called Kingdomtide. In others, Ascension and All-Saints Days are celebrated. In the cycle of the church year and the use of music in this cycle, it seems some emphasis should be given to God, The Creator. Music, in addition to speaking to our innermost convictions, is a vehicle for creativity and the building of fellowship.

This section of the book looks at music in the church school as a recreating force. It shows how music can combine with other creative activities.

The experience of the Christian is an experience of recreation, of newness, of novelty. Music can be a means of keeping the Christian experience fresh and vital.

A. MUSIC FOR THE VERY YOUNG CHILD

Music has the wonderful feature of belonging to all ages. Even the very young child in the Nursery department can experience the delights of music.

Music for the one and two year old child should never be organized. It should be spontaneous, simple melodies about familiar subjects. No piano or accompaniment is needed for these simple melodies. A clear, untrained voice is easiest for the very young child to imitate and imitation is exactly what the first efforts at singing are. These very young children are just beginning to experiment with songs. What a wonderful opportunity you have to encourage it!

The Church School class is the perfect setting for the kind of spontaneous singing that is so valuable to very young children. The teacher of this age group should have a repertoire of very short, simple songs ready to sing on a moment's notice. The teacher can sing, "I can help. I can help pick up toys" and the children, joining in, will not only be finding their singing voices but will also be forming valuable habits of spontaneous singing.

The teacher can sing, "This is the way we wash our hands, wash our hands, wash our hands". Children enjoy repeating one little phrase many times and the shorter the song, the easier for the child.

The teacher has many opportunities for free and spontaneous singing. She can sing a welcome as the children enter. He can sing a thank-you to God before cookies. He can sing songs to accompany the children's playing. She can sing about the pitter-patter of the rain or simply sing, "God cares about you."

In addition to these short melodies children can be given experiences in rhythm at this early age. Records should be used frequently in the Church school class. The teacher can march or sway or dance spontaneously with the children to the music.

The simple act of bouncing a child on your knee or foot as you sing is another excellent way to teach rhythm.

This is the age for children to begin having good, happy experiences with music. Free and unconventional singing-talk should be a happy part of your Church school class.

Finger Games for the Very Young Child

One of the first rhythmic actions of a child is clapping pat-a-cake. This enjoyment of making finger pictures can carry over into church school. In the following finger-chants the teacher says the verses and makes the motions. If the child is interested he joins in, thus learning them in time. No attempt should be made to teach them rigidly.

THE FINGER FAMILY'S GOOD MORNING

Beginning with the thumb, each finger in turn bows "good morning" to everyone.

Mother finger says, "Good morning, Good morning, Good morning to you."
Father finger says, "Good morning, Good morning, Good morning to you."
Brother finger says, "Good morning, Good morning, Good morning to you."
Sister finger says, "Good morning, Good morning, Good morning to you."
Baby finger says, "Good morning, Good morning, Good morning to you."

The "Good mornings" should be well accented to give the rhythm with a nod of the head and bowing of finger people.

THE CLOCK

"Tick, tock, tick, tock
Tick, tock" says the clock.
What is it time to do?

The hand sways from the wrist like a clock pendulum, fingers up. The clock tells the children when it is time to do a task. For example, "Time to put toys away"; "Time to put on our coats".

THE BIRDS NEST

Here is a nest all made of hay. (cup left hand like a nest)
Here the little birdies lay. (use fingers of right hand as birds)
Someday they will fly away. (fingers fly off into air)

THE RAIN SONG

(Hands on table. Separate fingers make pitter-patter of raindrops. Doubled up fingers into a fist with knuckles rolling back and forth on table make the thunder.)

Pitter, Patter raindrops falling.
Pitter, Patter all around
Listen, listen all you children
To the Pitter, Patter sound.
Rumble, Rumble goes the thunder.
Rumble, Rumble all around.
Listen, listen all you children
To the Rumble, Rumble sound.

SONGS FOR 3, 4, and 5 YEAR OLDS

Singing talk should continue into this age group and a child should be creating songs about himself and the things that go on in his world. This is a wonderful experience of creativity, telling how he/she feels and what the world is like. The more frequent the periods of informal singing the better. Children should sing as they go about playing in the different centers of the classroom, using music in a functional way, just as folk music was originally used.

More organized experiences of music can begin at this age too. Begin with songs that have been written about the child and his/her world—singing, jumping, action songs; songs about dressing; animal songs; travel songs about boats and trains and airplanes; songs about the weather and the seasons. Small children love very rhythmic songs. Songs whose range does not exceed more than 6 or 7 notes somewhere between middle and high C usually work best. Short songs (two or three lines) can be learned more quickly. Longer songs with a great deal of repetition are also enjoyed.

Encourage children to create their own songs about things they are studying. They can make up a song about playing together, about ways to help Mother and Father, about what Jesus was like as a little boy, about the beautiful, wonderful summertime. Encouraging every child to contribute will make your music a natural, spontaneous thing rather than a structured activity carried on by the teacher.

In this age group too, the teacher should make use of spontaneous singing. He/she can, for example, sing directions for activities.

MORE IDEAS ON MUSIC WITH YOUNG CHILDREN

Martin Luther is credited with saying that the way to teach songs was to teach the children and they, in turn would teach the elders. Let's look at some more ideas about using music with children.

The real secret of using music in the classroom lies in its correlation with the curriculum. Two questions that we must constantly keep in mind are:

1. Is it appropriate for the age group I am teaching?
2. Does the music lend itself to the subject matter of the lesson?

A child should always be able to grasp the total meaning of a song. Children can comprehend a song about washing their hands but not comprehend one about washing their sins away, an idea which is too abstract for their level of thinking. "Being saved" gives the young child trouble too. Some of the gospel songs for children have this disadvantage. Many of these songs have such a strong rhythmic pattern that children love and respond to, that I sometimes go ahead and use them and change the words or use only a part of them.

In addition to songs in the curriculum, sing songs about the seasons and sometimes sing just pure nonsense songs to create the atmosphere of relaxed and natural singing. Enthusiasm and interest on the part of the teacher are more important than vocal training. Singing time should be a joyous occasion. If the children seem disinterested and restless, recheck your own enthusiasm, method of presentation and choice of material.

Music adds variety to the class, edifies the material and allows for creativity and it also inspires. Inspiration, as you know, is the keystone of successful teaching.

B. SINGING WITH PUPPETS

What a lot of fun it is to sing along with puppets. I have found many times that young children who do not seem to show much interest in singing along with the teacher will perk up immediately if a puppet leads the singing. I have a small hand puppet with a happy lion face that is a beloved song leader in our nursery class. When he leaves the class the children kiss him and shake his hand and tell him to "keep singing" (sometimes he gets shy in front of the children and hides and won't sing). He is becoming worn and one round, felt paw is missing, but he is a very real, loved person to these small children. I picked this puppet up at a church bazaar. I also have a finger puppet of a smiling frog that I use when singing with young children. He came from the Dime store. Some of the young children were frightened when I put the hand puppet on them but the little finger puppet is just their size and they move him and dance him and hop him with delight.

With a little older child it is fun to make singing puppets.

Cut two pieces of material big enough to fit over the hand.

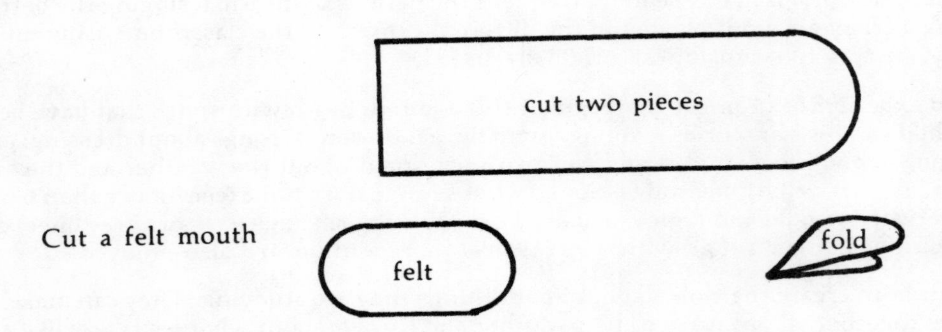

Insert the mouth between the two sides. Sew in place. Put on a button eye.

You have a singing puppet. Work with the thumb for the jaw and other fingers for the upper mouth.

There are many fun experiences for using these puppets. A group of children, each with a puppet, can get behind a stage or table. A record of singing (such as "Joy is Like the Rain") is played. The children's puppets move their mouths and bodies to pantomime the singing.

A fun idea is to have a class of children tape songs they know. Then, playing back the tape, use the puppets as singers.

C. MUSIC AND SCRIPTURE CARDS

"Tell Me the Stories of Jesus" is one of our most beloved hymns for children and may be found in most standard hymnals.

This song is sung so much that many of us have ceased to listen to the words, but they can be an excellent teaching resource on the life of Jesus.

Use the Scripture Cards by the American Bible Society. A packet of approximately 35 colored cards featuring the line drawings of Annie Vallotton from the GOOD NEWS FOR MODERN MAN version of the bible can be ordered from Griggs Educational Service.

After the children have sung "Tell Me the Stories of Jesus" let them select cards which accompany the words. How many "scenes by the wayside" and "tales of the sea" can they identify from the cards? What "stories of Jesus" are illustrated on the cards?

After selecting the cards the group can share the ones they chose.

For the second verse let the children find the card labeled, "Let the Children Come." I heard Annie Vollotton say once that this is the one illustration she would change for American children. Ask the class if they can guess why. If you look closely you will see one child is playing with some snails. For American children, she said, she would make it kittens.

Identify the card "God Bless the King" to illustrate the third verse of the song. The class can read the backs of the two cards used to illustrate the second and third verses and compare the Scripture with the hymn.

D. ART AND MUSIC

There are a variety of ways to combine music with art expressions and double the creative experience. The simplest method is the literal illustration of a hymn.

"All Things Bright and Beautiful" is an excellent example of the type of hymn that begs to be illustrated: *the little flowers, the little birds, the glowing colors, the purple mountains, the rivers, the gardens,* hold promise of a bright, colorful Spring picture.

ALL THINGS BRIGHT AND BEAUTIFUL

Cecil Alexander — Old English Melody

Chorus:
All things bright and beautiful, All creatures great and small,
All things wise and wonderful: the Lord God made them all.

Verses:
Each little flower that opens, Each little bird that sings:
He made their glowing colors, He made their tiny wings.

The purple-headed mountain, The river running by,
The sunset and the morning That brightens up the sky.

The cold wind in the winter, The pleasant summer sun,
The ripe fruits in the garden; He made them every one.

He gave us eyes to see them, And lips that we might tell
How great is God Almighty, Who has made all things well.

Students can work individually or they can work as a group on a large mural. Excellent instructions for the use of tempera paints, water colors and tissue paper collages are given in the book, CREATIVE ACTIVITIES IN CHURCH EDUCATION by Patricia Griggs. Any or all of these media would work well with this hymn.

Mood Painting

A more mature use of artistic interpretation of hymns would be a mood painting. In this instance a student would listen to or sing a hymn and then illustrate the mood the hymn provoked. The use of color here is most obvious and finger paints would be a useful media.

Hymns such as "I Know that my Redeemer Lives" or "Come Thou Disconsolate" or "Holy, Holy, Holy" would work well with this type of mood painting.

In this type of creative expression there can be no wrong response. It is how the person feels that is illustrated.

Another type of mood painting would be a line drawing using black felt-tipped pens on white poster paper. After a hymn is sung or while listening to it being sung, the student uses lines to express the sweep of the phrases or the jagged contour of a melody, emphasizing how the song makes him feel.

Mood painting works best with older students.

Artistic Expressions with Youth

Refer to the hymn "O Young and Fearless Prophet" (found in most hymnals). Distribute the words to this hymn. Youth are to communicate non-verbally their own response to the hymn by sketching, painting or drawing the main idea they identify in the hymn. They may use any media with which they feel comfortable.

Afterward the class can compare pictures. Since there are several main ideas you will probably find a variety of themes in the pictures. This should provoke discussion. It is an interesting experience sometimes to just read the words of a hymn that the class is used to singing.

Another idea that works effectively with youth is to distribute hymnals and ask each student to illustrate any hymn he wishes on large paper. Work should be done individually. Then, the group selects one (without knowing whose) and discusses what they think the painting is saying. The artist may respond. This process can then be followed with other paintings of the group.

Using Art to Teach a Song

A large flip chart with illustrations to accompany the words is a quick and effective way to teach a song, especially if you are teaching it by rote. These illustrations can be done by the teacher or by the students.

A flannelboard is another good teaching device. As words to a hymn are learned, pieces can be added to the flannelboard to reinforce the learning.

Montage

An effective contemporary montage can be used to illustrate the hymn "Where Cross the Crowded Ways of Life."

WHERE CROSS THE CROWDED WAYS OF LIFE

Frank Mason North — From William Gardiner's Sacred Melodies

Where cross the crowded ways of life,
Where sound the cries of race and clan,
Above the noise of selfish strife,
We hear Thy voice, O Son of man!

In haunts of wretchedness and need,
On shadowed thresholds dark with fears,
From paths where hide the lures of greed,
We catch the vision of Thy tears.

From tender childhood's helplessness,
From woman's grief, man's burdened toil,
From famished souls, from sorrow's stress,
Thy heart has never known recoil.

The cup of water given for Thee
Still hold the freshness of Thy grace;
Yet long these multitudes to see
The sweet compassion of Thy face.

You will need:
- a collection of picture magazines
- scissors
- glue
- poster paper
- felt-tipped pens

Read or sing the hymn and think about the words. Working as a group, cut pictures from the magazines to illustrate the hymn. The hymn is rich in suggestions of current events. The words are extremely provocative and contemporary. The students paste the pictures in any way, spontaneously, on the poster board. They may cut out words in addition to pictures or write in their own words. When the montage is completed students may explain why they choose their particular picture or pictures. This can produce a very creative, meaningful piece of art work.

Sculpture

WE BEAR THE STRAIN OF EARTHLY CARE

Ozora Davis — Carl Glazer

We bear the strain of earthly care,
But bear it not alone.
Beside us walks our Brother Christ
And makes our tasks His own.
Through din of market, whirl of wheels
and thrust of driving trade.
We follow where the Master leads,
Serene and unafraid.

Select a large variety of different type material and pile it all on a central table. Some suggestions:
small tools, pieces of machinery different sizes and shapes of wood,
tin cans, screening material, toothpicks, bottlecaps, wire

Students are creatively to construct a "scripture" depicting the theme of this hymn. This could also be an activity for use in a learning center.

Banners

BREAK THOU THE BREAD OF LIFE

Mary Lathbury William Sherwin

Break Thou the Bread of Life
Dear Lord to me,
As Thou didst break the loaves Beside the sea;
Beyond the sacred page I seek Thee Lord;
My spirit pants for Thee, O living Word!

Bless Thou the truth, dear Lord To me, to me.
As Thou didst bless the bread by Galilee;
Then shall all bondage cease, All fetters fall;
And I shall find my peace, My All in All.

Here is a hymn rich in symbolism and word pictures of symbols. This would be an excellent hymn to illustrate with banners. Have students draw a symbol they discover from the hymn; "fetters of bondage", "Bread of life," "Living Word". Cut the symbol out of felt and mount it on a piece of felt or burlap. This can be an individual project or a project for a group of students working together.

Another hymn to use in creating symbols on a banner is "The Church's One Foundation."

Slides

Slides can be used to illustrate hymns.

THIS IS MY FATHER'S WORLD

Maltbie Babcock Franklin Sheppard

This is my Father's world and to my listening ears,
All nature sings, and round me rings The music of the spheres,
This is my Father's world; I rest me in the thought
Of rocks and trees, of skies and seas; His hand the wonders wrought.

This is my Father's world, The birds their carols raise,
The morning light, the lily white, Declare their Maker's praise.
This is my Father's world; He shines in all that's fair;
In the rustling grass I hear Him pass, He speaks to me everywhere.

This is my Father's world, O let me ne 'er forget
That though the wrong seems oft so strong, God is the Ruler yet.
This is my Father's world; Why should my heart be sad?
The Lord is King; let the heavens ring! God reigns; let the earth be glad!

"Rocks and trees—skies and seas—birds and grass—" all offer possibilities for pictures.

Using a 35mm camera and color film, students can shoot pictures to illustrate the words. This is a good project because it makes students aware of their particular surroundings as "God's world". After the slides are developed they can be shown as the class sings.

Another possibility is for the students to create their own slides with a box of Write-On slides and a set of projection pencils. These slides have the advantage of being available immediately without having to wait for them to be developed.

E. MUSIC AND DRAMA

Role Playing

Trying drama with music is another way to make the study of hymns more meaningful.

Role-play is a method in which a situation in human relationships is acted out spontaneously, followed by a discussion of what happened and why. Students put themselves into a situation, suggested by a hymn and try to experience how a person in that situation might feel and act.

I WOULD BE TRUE

Step 1: Sing together the hymn "I Would Be True"

Step 2: From class discussion pick out an idea, suggested by the hymn for role-playing. For example, the phrase "I would be friend of all—the foe, the friendless."

Step 3: Apply this idea to your community, your class, your situation. For example, perhaps a refugee family has come into your community. This might suggest a role-playing situation correlating with the words in which the "friendless" are met by a student. Develop the idea with the class. Encourage the students to suggest ideas.

Step 4: Choose persons from the class to act the roles. Suggestions for playing the role are never offered by the teacher. They grow out of the student's interpretation.

Step 5: Act out the situation spontaneously.

Step 6: Following the role-play the class discusses the situation (never the acting). Did the characters act in a manner that was in keeping with the theme of the hymn "I Would Be True?"

Tableau

A tableau is a living picture. Students create a scene and hold it silent and motionless as the verses of a hymn are sung. Some sort of framing should enclose the picture and there should be some means of concluding the picture, such as drawing curtains or drapes.

"We Would See Jesus" is an excellent hymn to use with a tableau because each of the five verses of the hymn suggests a different picture.

Verse 1 suggests a Christmas tableau with a manger, shepherds and kings.

At the conclusion of this verse the curtains should be drawn and the second picture formed.

Verse 2 suggests Jesus as a young boy helping in his father Joseph's carpenter shop.
Verse 3 pictures Jesus as a young man teaching and preaching.
Verse 4 shows Jesus healing.
Verse 5 suggests an Easter morning scene or a contemporary scene in which Jesus is calling followers today.

This is a good project to use for a class studying the Life and Ministry of Jesus.

"We Would See Jesus"

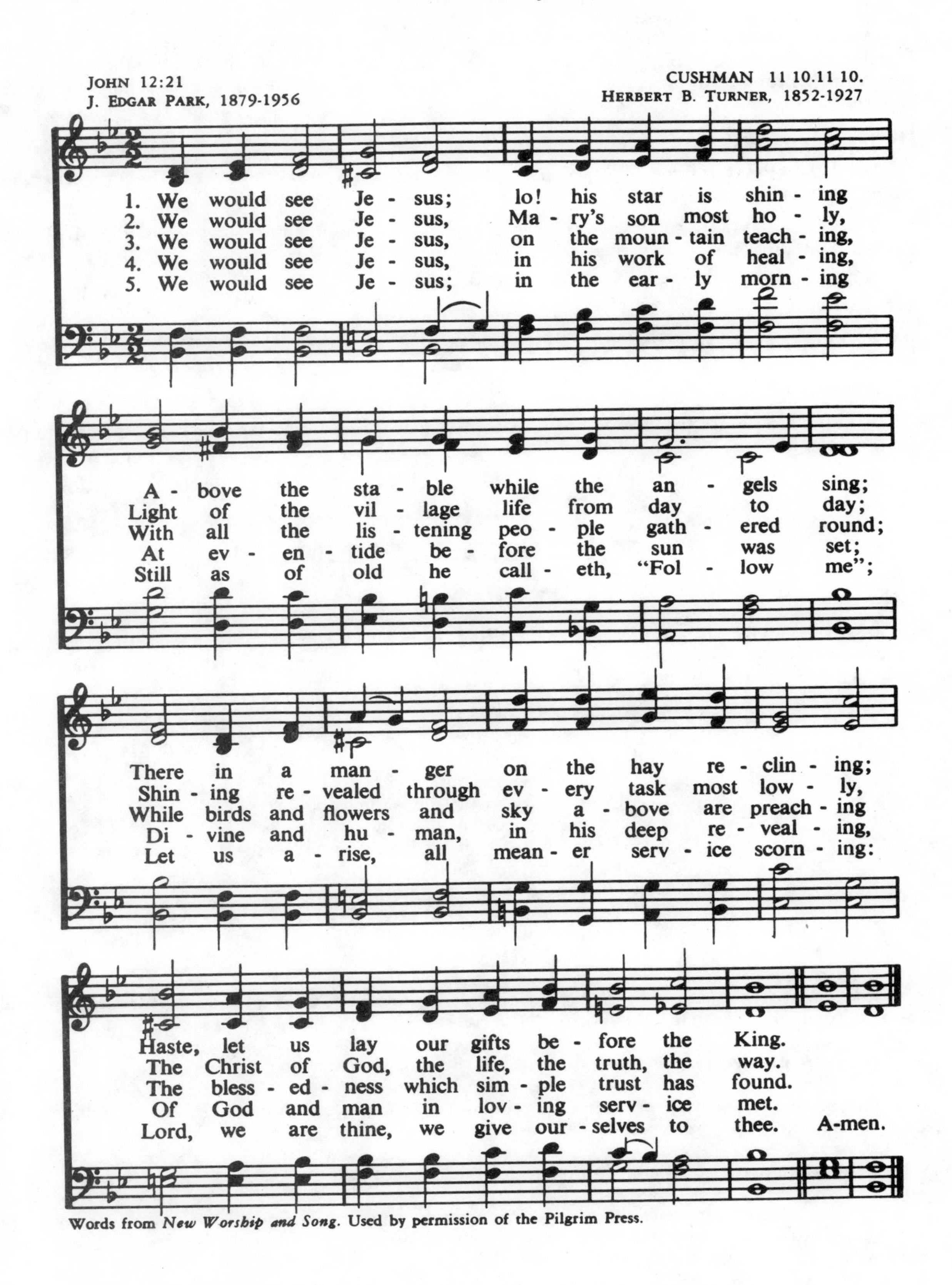

A more modern song that can be used in the same way is "Possibly, Probably," by Avery and Marsh from the book, THE AVERY AND MARSH SONGBOOK, Proclamation Productions. In the verses of this song Jesus is seen as 1. a baby, 2. a student, 3. a young man, 4. a preacher, 5. a leader, 6. a rebel.

Hymn Charades

For a class that has done a lot of work with hymns and has sung a number of them together you might try this idea:

Divide the class into small groups. Each group chooses a hymn and then pantomimes the title in charade fashion. The other groups try to guess the name of the hymn.

A variation of this game is to pantomime the content or purpose of a hymn and let the others guess what it is.

F. CREATIVE WRITING: LITANY

Another art form that can be used in the study of music is creative writing.

A litany is a prayer that has a chorus or refrain that is repeated after each sentence or group of sentences. This repeated response can be sung.

A group of second and third graders wrote this litany of thanks. Their response was sung to this simple tune.

We Thank you God

First the children learned to sing this refrain. Then we went spontaneously around the group, each child offering one sentence. After each sentence the entire group sang the refrain. This is what they said:

God gives us sunshine and rain
  We thank you God.
God gives us trees and bushes and flowers
  We thank you God.
God gives us food and the animals too.
  We thank you God
God plans for us to have family and friends (teachers response)
  We thank you God
God is good to us every minute
  We thank you God
God loves us all
  We thank you God

Take the words of a hymn such as "How Firm a Foundation". Look up the Scriptural background for the hymn. In this case, 2 Timothy 2:19; Hebrews 13:5; Isaiah 43:1-2.

Write creatively your feelings about what the words are saying for you today.

This project will work best with older students. You might also consider it for a learning project or an intergenerational project.

Write your own songs and hymns.

It is an exciting experience to write your own hymns and songs. Sometimes a student may write words and music of an original hymn to culminate a unit of study. Usually, however, the students take a familiar melody and write their own words.

A group of 10 and 11 year old students studying the life of Paul wrote the following songs:

FRIENDS OF PAUL

(They used the following words from their study book as inspiration, "When you have made a friend and then begin to meet his friends you're really getting well acquainted." Their Scripture references were Acts 9:9-19 and Acts 9:26-28 and the tune they chose was "Old MacDonald Had a Farm.")

Chorus: Friends of Paul we all should know E-I-E-I-O
Without their help he could not grow E-I-E-I-O

Verse 1: Ananias brave, Ananias free
Ananias helping Paul to see (repeat chorus)

Verse 2: Barnabas stately, Barnabas tall,
Barnabas going to preach with Paul (repeat chorus)

Verse 3: Enter Aquila, wife, Priscilla
Shared with Paul their shop and villa (repeat chorus)

Verse 4: Timothy young, Timothy fair
Accompanying Paul everywhere (repeat chorus)

Their second song "Brave Apostle Paul" was based on the action song "The Noble Duke of York".

BRAVE APOSTLE PAUL

Verse 1: The brave Apostle Paul
He faced his hardships all
He walked 3,000 Roman miles (stand up)
And then walked back again (sit down)
And when he was up, he was up (stand up)
And when he was down, he was down (sit down)
And when he was only half way up (crouch between up and down)
He was neither up (stand up)
nor down (sit down)

Verse 2: Repeat actions. Sing very slowly.

Verse 2: The brave Apostle Paul
He faced his hardships all
Often he traveled on the sea
And four times his ship went down.
And when he was up, he was up,
And when he was down, he was down,
And when he was only half way up
He was neither up
Nor down.

Verse 3: Same motions very fast.

The brave Apostle Paul
He faced his hardships all
Beatened, imprisoned and threatened with death
And still he traveled on
And when he was up, he was up,
And when he was down, he was down.
And when he was only half way up,
He was neither up
Nor down.

Encourage your students to try their hand at some writing. This might be an activity that two or three students working together could best accomplish.

G. SINGING GAMES

Does your church enjoy the benefits of a community-wide ecumenical vacation church school? This can be a very rewarding experience and music and singing games are a wonderful means of joining children from varying backgrounds together.

In addition to songs in the curriculum, fellowship can be built with nonsense songs, rounds, camp songs and singing games.

Folk songs are usually a good common denominator. You might begin with a song such as "I've Been Working on the Railroad". In the first section of the song have the students act out any sort of work rhythm (hammering, digging, tugging, all in rhythm.) Large balls may be bounced in rhythm to the music of the "Dinah" verse. In the "Fe-Fi-Fiddle-i-o" section the ball may be alternately bounced and thrown into the air on the strong beat of the music.

"Whoopi-Ti-Yi-Yo" is one of the best known of the Western folk songs. For rhythmic activity students can slow gallop around the room swinging imaginary lariats over their heads. Using wood-block accompaniment makes an interesting horses-hoofs sound.

"The Muffin Man" is another folk song that is usually familiar to students. To make a game of it blindfold one student. The entire group sings the first verse. On the second verse one of the group sings alone. The blindfolded student tries to guess who the soloist is. If the guess is correct, the soloist is blind-folded and the game continues.

If you have access to marionettes they are fun to use with the folk song "Dem Bones." Students operate the strings making a quick gesture with the part of the anatomy mentioned in the song.

Other types of singing games include follow-the-leader songs in which a leader performs an action to be imitated by the rest of the students. "Here We Go Round The Mulberry Bush" is an example of this type of game.

Word-play songs are favorites. These usually require making appropriate sounds, answering questions or echoing words "B-i-n-g-o" is an example of this type of song, as is "Who Did?"

Motion songs which involve specific, often traditional gestures and motions to be performed while singing are fun. "She'll be Coming Round the Mountain" is an example of this type of song.

Clapping, jumping, acting out the words, falling down, making animal sounds, echoing words—are all characteristics of favorite singing games of children.

The library is a good place to start looking for these songs and games. Scout song books, camp song books, folk-song books, books on nursery rhymes are all good resources for Vacation Church School music. The book, THE GOOD TIMES SONGBOOK compiled by James Leisy, Abingdon Press, is another helpful resource.

CODA:

The following song summarizes the philosophy of this book. A vital, enthusiastic Christian just has to burst out sometimes with "Hip, hip hooray and Hallelujah!" And what can express this sentiment better than music?

SOMETIMES

A SONG FOR A HAPPY OCCASION dedicated to the
Ross B. Decker family, all of them
RICHARD AVERY
DONALD MARSH
Eb Cm Fm Bb7 Eb
I've got a word to say to the Fa-ther: "Hip, hip, hoo-
Cm Fm Bb7 Eb Cm Fm
ray and Ha-le-lu-jah!" Most of the time I just ne-ver
Bb7 Eb Bb Ebm Eb7
bo-ther, Poop poop-a-doop I'm much too bu-sy but
Ab Ab Fm
* Some-times when the sun shines bright and Some-times
Some-times af--ter T. V. view---ing,Some-times
Some-times when we're all O. K. and Some-times
Fm Fm D° D°
when the moon's a sight and Some-times when the stars are
af--ter chick-en stew--ing Some-times af--ter hair sham-
when we laugh and play and Some-times on a ho----li--
D° Bb9 Bb9
right and Some-times all the day and night, yes,
poo--ing Some-times af---ter air-plane glue---ing
day and Some-times when we bow and pray, yes,
Eb Cm Ab Bb Eb
Some-times, some-times I've got to say: "Hip, hip, hoo-
Eb B7 Bb7 Eb Bb7 Eb
ray and Ha-le-lu-jah! Thank you, God, for ev--'ry-thing."
* From this point it's fun to divide with Dad on the first "Sometime...", Mom on the second, Daughter on the third, and Son on the last, or some other division by age or sex. How about a family anthem?